IMMERSION
Bible Studies

EZEKIEL
DANIEL

Praise for IMMERSION

"IMMERSION BIBLE STUDIES is a powerful tool in helping readers to hear God speak through Scripture and to experience a deeper faith as a result."
    Adam Hamilton, author of *24 Hours That Changed the World*

"IMMERSION BIBLE STUDIES is a godsend for participants who desire sound Bible study yet feel they do not have large amounts of time for study and preparation. IMMERSION is concise. It is brief but covers the material well and leads participants to apply the Bible to life. IMMERSION is a wonderful resource for today's church."
    Larry R. Baird, senior pastor of Trinity Grand Island United Methodist Church

"This beautiful series helps readers become fluent in the words and thoughts of God, for purposes of illumination, strength building, and developing a closer walk with the One who loves us so."
    Laurie Beth Jones, author of *Jesus, CEO* and *The Path*

"The IMMERSION BIBLE STUDIES series is no less than a game changer. It ignites the purpose and power of Scripture by showing us how to do more than just know God or love God; it gives us the tools to love like God as well."
    Shane Stanford, author of *You Can't Do Everything . . . So Do Something*

IMMERSION
Bible Studies

EZEKIEL
DANIEL

Carlyle Fielding Stewart, III

Abingdon Press

Nashville

EZEKIEL, DANIEL
IMMERSION BIBLE STUDIES
by Carlyle Fielding Stewart, III

Copyright © 2013 by Abingdon Press

Library of Congress Cataloging-in-Publication Data

Stewart, Carlyle Fielding, 1951-
  Ezekiel, Daniel / Carlyle Fielding Stewart, III.
    pages cm. — (Immersion Bible studies)
    ISBN 978-1-4267-1638-6 (pbk., unsewn,/adhesive bound : alk. paper) 1. Bible.
Ezekiel—Textbooks. 2. Bible. Daniel—Textbooks. I. Title.
  BS1545.55.S74 2013
  224'.406—dc23
                                                                        2013027842

Editor: Marvin W. Cropsey
Leader Guide Writer: Pamela Dilmore

13 14 15 16 17 18 19 20 21 22—10 9 8 7 6 5 4 3 2 1

Manufactured in the United States of America

Contents

Review Team

Immersion Bible Studies

*A fresh new look at the Bible, from beginning to end,
and what it means in your life.*

Welcome to Immersion!

We've asked some of the leading Bible scholars, teachers, and pastors to help us with a new kind of Bible study. Immersion remains true to Scripture but always asks, "Where are you in your life? What do you struggle with? What makes you rejoice?" Then it helps you read the Scriptures to discover their deep, abiding truths. Immersion is about God and God's Word, and it is also about you—not just your thoughts, but your feelings and your faith.

In each study you will prayerfully read the Scripture and reflect on it. Then you will engage it in three ways:

Claim Your Story
> Through stories and questions, think about your life, with its struggles and joys.

Enter the Bible Story
> Explore Scripture and consider what God is saying to you.

Live the Story
> Reflect on what you have discovered, and put it into practice in your life.

IMMERSION makes use of an exciting new translation of Scripture, the Common English Bible (CEB). The CEB and IMMERSION BIBLE STUDIES will offer adults:

- the emotional expectation to find the love of God
- the rational expectation to find the knowledge of God
- reliable, genuine, and credible power to transform lives
- clarity of language

Whether you are using the Common English Bible or another translation, IMMERSION BIBLE STUDIES will offer a refreshing plunge into God's Word, your life, and your life with God.

1.

Finally Comes the Prophet: The Call and Commissioning of Ezekiel

Ezekiel 1–3

Claim Your Story

One minute, two children are happily playing; the next minute, they are roiling in such a noisy conflict that their mother runs over to see whatever is the matter. She asks each child, "What is the matter with you? Why can't you two play nicely and get along?" Then comes the punishment. Mother says, "Since you can't follow the rules and behave yourselves, you have to go to your rooms and consider what you have done." The children are separated and left alone.

When a teenage student and a school chum are planning a report for a science or history class, they disagree about some fact or about their duties. Heat, not light, comes from the debate. Anger mounts. Neither one wants to give in, so one storms away, leaving both to wonder what just happened and how they separated from their best friend. Each student is isolated.

Since we all—even adults—have difficulty growing up, we continue to have occasions when the pieces to the puzzle of life just don't fit. Perhaps God hasn't answered a fervent prayer and we are angry and confused. Surely God can see the wisdom and righteousness of whatever we asked. How can God be so insensitive and uncaring? You are exiled from God's presence.

Then comes the question, "What do I do now?"

Enter the Bible Story

The Reality of Exile: But How Can We Sing the Lord's Song in a Strange Land?

The story of Ezekiel occurred during a time of crisis in the lives of God's people. The noise and trouble of their exile eclipsed their memory of God's repeated promises of hope.

Two basic types of crises confronted them. There was a *personal crisis*, which was related to a person's dislocation and estrangement from other individuals in his or her community. Such crises often resulted in personal alienation and insecurity, which ruptured one's vital connections to others in the community, including family. The second was a *social crisis* that affected groups of people. Thus, certain groups were disconnected from other groups based on race, class, religious beliefs and practice, ethnicity, gender, nationality, or some other factor.

Whether individual or collective, personal or social, the result of such alienation is a form of exile where individuals and social groups need to find ways to belong in the larger society. A central purpose of human community is to create and find places to be somebody, to experience the feeling of home in society, and to establish a sense of belonging in the world. Exile can be the prolonged condition of isolation from others, stemming from these various forms of crises. Persons in exile long to hear words of hope and to receive compassion from others. They desire spokespersons who can nurture their needs and address their ultimate concerns as human beings. Justice and righteousness are at the heart of their concerns.

The need for belonging often requires a messenger who will speak on behalf of the exiled and the oppressed, a person or persons who will tell their story and help them move beyond the various forms of estrangement that have been imposed upon them and insulated them from the sources of life and hope in society. The messenger often speaks to their deep pain and suffering and holds before them the possibilities of restoration and renewal that mark the beginning of their return to God. We all long for home. All we need is someone to remind us of home and lead us back.

The Jews in the Book of Ezekiel experienced personal and social crisis because of their three deportations to Babylon. Among the first deportees was Daniel in 605 B.C. The second deportation included Ezekiel in 597 B.C. The third, to which Ezekiel ultimately pointed, was in 586 B.C. when Jerusalem and its Temple were destroyed.[1] Estranged from their homeland, the Jews felt additional alienation because their exile was thought to be punishment from God for turning away and disobeying God's commandments. Deeply forlorn because of their new social situation, the people were in desperate need of a messenger who would give them hope.

Our lesson today introduces us to Ezekiel, the messenger called and commissioned to speak warning and hope to the people of God. Ezekiel heard the word of God through divine visions and delivered the messages to a people in exile. Much of that message recounts the many ways the people have sinned against God and have been led astray by various leaders. After years in exile, the people finally heard from God through Ezekiel, whose ultimate message of hope and restoration gave them confidence in the future.

God desires our spiritual restoration. God provides redemption and hope for the people of God, which is a message often lost in the confusion and mayhem of our various forms of personal and social alienation. God loves us and wants to restore us to a time when God's name and presence were honored and people were strengthened and renewed because of that divine intervention.

On the one hand, the Jewish people were individually estranged from God due to their personal abandonment of faith. On the other hand, they were alienated collectively as a faith community by their theological and geographical displacement from the familiar moorings of their beloved faith traditions and cherished homeland. They might have asked questions like, How can we sing the songs of Zion when we have lost our God and our land? How can we sing songs of hope and redemption when our lives have been drowned out by the dissonance of exile? How can we sing the songs of our future restoration when our captors devastated us?

The Book of Ezekiel tells the story of a priest, prophet, and street preacher called by God to address both the personal and the social crises of his community. The people longed to go back home. But as novelist Thomas Wolfe reveals, once separated—whether from Lybia Hill or the City of David—"you can't go home again." Some of the people adjusted to life in exile and lost their songs of joy. They would never sing happily or expectantly again. Many had lost hope of ever returning home. Others dismissed their right of return. Others completely capitulated themselves to their situation and accepted it as a permanent state of defeat. Still others held out hope for restoration and redemption but remained a silent minority.

The primary question then is, "How could we possibly sing the LORD's song on foreign soil?" (Psalm 137:4). If we can recapture our ability to sing the songs of Zion, we can lift our spirits beyond the immediate miseries of exile to new visions of God's future redemption and restoration. How can we have hope and joy when we have lost everything familiar to us such as our faith, our freedom, our future, our property, our possessions, and our promises? We have been robbed not only of our dignity but also our sense of "somebodiness" as a promised people.

> The task that was assigned to Ezekiel was to prophesy to the exiles of Judah, who had been carried away into captivity in distant Babylon. It was an audience close to despair, asking why this disaster had come on them and where God was in the middle of their personal holocaust.[2]

Ezekiel also had to juxtapose these oracles with a message of redemption and salvation for a people who had almost lost all hope of ever being restored by God. He had to remind the people that even though they felt abandoned and alone, God is still close to them and still determined to save and restore them. Even though he was delivering the message of God, the prophet risked danger to his own life because the people were comfortable in their estranged condition and might be unreceptive to his message.

Tamara Eskenazi describes exile as not simply being homeless; exile means knowing that you do have a home, but the home has been taken over by enemies. It means having deep roots in one's homeland but being taken from home, carried far away, and exposed to the cold and pain in an alien world. Exile means knowing where you are but lamenting that you can't go back home, not yet.[3] God called Ezekiel because God desires to meet people where they are, which is often at their point of greatest need. God's word is creative and powerful and moves the people from exile toward redemption and salvation. Knowing this, the exiles *could* sing the Lord's song in a strange land if they had faith in God's redemption and deliverance.

Living as a Christian in modern society can be a form of exile because of the feelings of aloneness and our disconnection from the trappings of modern culture. We lose hope of ever belonging in the world, yet we know God loved the world. We see these various forms of exile in various faith communities, in the modern church, and in the larger society. Katheryn Pfisterer Darr reminds us that "Ezekiel 37:11 attests to the sense of resignation experienced by at least some of the exiles after years in Babylonia: 'Our bones are dried up, and our hope is lost; we are cut off completely.' We should not suppose that all of the deportees experienced the same reactions throughout the entire exilic period. While some clung with tenacity to their distinct ethnic identity, others probably assimilated into Babylonian culture rapidly. While some struggled mightily to maintain faith in Yahweh, others probably shifted their devotion to Babylonian deities."[4]

By recalling our own feelings of estrangement or feelings of pain, isolation, and discomfort, we can sense what being in exile really means and get a sense of the exilic mindsets and feelings of the people of Ezekiel's time. They were estranged from their homeland, their religious traditions, their families, and their communities. Thus, they were cut off from the vitalizing forces that make for human wholeness and completeness. Ezekiel 37:11 says, "Our bones are dried up, and our hope has perished. We are completely finished." However, you can find hope and faith that God still has the power to redeem and restore the people.

The Calling and First Vision of Ezekiel: God Gets Ezekiel's Attention with a Divine Vision Plan

Ezekiel 1

God called and commissioned Ezekiel to speak urgently to the problems leading to and resulting from their exile in Babylon. The messenger must vigorously speak to the theological and practical reasons for their exile. He must describe the nature of their alienated condition and how it dissipates their hope and increases their crisis of faith, causing them to turn inward and not outward toward God. He must proclaim God's corrective action to that condition and warn them of the disastrous results if that counsel goes unheeded. He must help them claim the redemptive possibilities of God amid their own human disabilities.

God was concerned about the people. God's love for them inspired God's search for and restoration of them. However sinful the people of God became, God did not delight in their prolonged estrangement and exile. Theologian Karl Barth reminds us that God finds us where we are, in our isolation and brokenness, the disruptions caused by our sinfulness.[5] Theologian and preacher John Wesley believed that he had to take the message of Christ's salvation to the people and not eternally wait for them to seek it amid the woeful conditions of their social and economic alienation.[6]

Wham! Out of nowhere came the divine vision plan. Weird and wonderful images from driving storms, great clouds flashing fire, four living creatures each with four faces and four wings set in a giant wheel, burst on Ezekiel with dazzling power that startled and throttled him. Even in this strange land, amid the seductive and captivating idolatries of Babylonian culture and power, God called forth such dazzling Mesopotamian pyrotechnics to subdue the people's complacency and remind them that God still had jurisdiction and could call down thunder and rain. God even burst open the heavens to remind the people of the universal reach of God's true sovereignty and power.

Do you actually think that I would forget about you, asked God in Ezekiel's vision, *that I am not paying attention to you? That I had disappeared completely from the face of this earth? You are still my people! I am still your God! There will be justice and righteousness. I will return to you and you will return to me.*

Across the Testaments

Visions

Visions from God awaken and motivate those privileged to receive them. The graphic value of divine vision as a catalyst for prophetic speech amid the sterility and monotony of life in exile is an important hallmark in Ezekiel's calling. We see these visions as radically other than the ordinary visions of daily life. Often, the routine of life conditions our ability to see things a certain way.

God's radical vision breaks in on Ezekiel in such a startling and bizarre manner that *the way* that vision was revealed is almost as important as *what* that vision revealed. It was a radical message of hope delivered in the form of a radical vision. Such outbreaks are so extraordinary that they confirm the presence of God and the power of God's calling of individuals for service.

Exodus 3 recalls Moses' call to service and his experience of a vision from God in the form of a burning bush. His calling and commissioning required that he go to one of the most powerful people on earth and speak a divine message of liberation for an oppressed people. Realizing the magnitude of this undertaking, Moses was frightened. The vision of the burning bush and the voice of God are what finally got his attention.

The Book of Revelation chronicles a similarly radical vision by the apostle who had been exiled on the Island of Patmos during a time of the early Christian movement's days of persecution. The apostle's message was a word of hope and warning to the seven churches and urged constant vigilance and watchfulness of the power of God to overcome a formidable enemy.

After being baptized by John the Baptist, Jesus experienced the Spirit of God descending like a dove and lightning and as a voice of heaven authenticating for him the divine source of his calling (Matthew 3:16).

Visions not only contain the imagery and language of God but also have sufficient power to galvanize and strengthen God's appointed messengers into critical actions of prophetic engagement that will criticize the status quo and energize the people for the common good.

God got the messenger's attention through this powerful divine vision. The messenger was both awed and amazed at God's artistic vision breaking in upon him like catastrophic storms and responds favorably to it. Now he must awaken and respond to this vision. The messenger realizes that it is no longer business as usual; God was seeking to restore God's people, hoping and trusting that they had learned the lessons of their past.

Ezekiel's Commissions: Ezekiel's Engagement With a Divine Action Plan
Ezekiel 2–3

To clearly hear God's radical calling through visions while in exile was not only shocking but also fascinating. The prophet heeded the call through the radical first vision and prepared to receive a word from God that he must take to the exiles.

The commission confirmed the authenticity of Ezekiel's divine calling as a spokesperson for God and confirmed the moral and spiritual authority in which the prophet walked and spoke as a servant of God to the exiles. If the divine vision involved a radical awakening to seeing and hearing from God about the nature of the prophetic assignment to the exiles, the divine commission confirmed his active engagement and participation in telling the people what God wants them to hear. Ezekiel was chosen for this prophetic task, and this commissioning involved three basic actions:

1) *Standing on Your Feet and Listening to God:* "Human one, stand on your feet, and I'll speak to you" (Ezekiel 2:1).

2) *Walking With Your Feet to the People of God:* "I'm sending you to the Israelites, a traitorous and rebellious people. They and their ancestors have been rebelling against me to this very day. I'm sending you to their hardheaded and hardhearted descendants" (verses 3-4).

3) *Staying on Your Feet and Speaking the Truth of God:* "Whether they listen or whether they refuse, since they are a household of rebels, they will know that a prophet has been among them" (verse 5).

God gave the prophet a strategic plan in the form of a vision. Now the strategic plan must be followed by an action plan formed by the prophet and the people.

Stand on Your Feet and Listen to God!

"Human one, stand on your feet, and I'll speak to you" (Ezekiel 2:1).

The moment of reckoning was upon Ezekiel. He saw the vision. He heard God's voice. Standing on one's feet meant assuming a vertical position of physical, moral, and spiritual uprightness and holy boldness; it meant taking a position of readiness to hear and receive that word. Standing on one's feet suggested an astute alertness to hear from God at a time when the oppression of exile had lowered the people's standing, slowed their response time and urgency in crisis, dulled their hearing, and crushed them to ground level. They could no longer bear the weight of being a chosen people. They said, "Our bones are dried up, and our hope has perished. We are completely finished" (37:11). They could neither live nor move.

Standing on one's feet in response to God and listening to learn what words of God to speak to the people required discipline and suggests that the prophet must have been among those who would be ready, steadfast, and forthright in doing God's work. No more lying down in the complacency of captivity! The prophet stood up and stood out to be counted to bring a word of hope and redemption to a people forlorn, and the people stood up in response to the prophet's message if they were to receive God's redemption and salvation. Standing up and listening to God was an important step in God's commissioning of Ezekiel. God sought to positively transform the woeful conditions of God's people into a spiritual, relational, and practical uprightness where they could once again stand tall in God's and their own eyes.

Walk With Your Feet to the People of God!

"I'm sending you to the Israelites, a traitorous and rebellious people. They and their ancestors have been rebelling against me to this very day. I'm sending you to their hardheaded and hardhearted descendants"

(2:3-4). Divine action plans for redemption and salvation require action heroes and heroines willing to go to the people and put forth the divine message even to ears that do not want to hear. Jesus said, "Let the person who has ears, hear" (Matthew 11:15). We must therefore go where we would not otherwise go and do what we would otherwise not do. Ezekiel's calling involved acts of hearing, seeing, and interpreting the visions of God. Ezekiel's commissioning involved standing, hearing, going, and speaking the word of God to the people of God.

Stay on Your Feet and *Speak* the Truth of God!
"And you will say to them: The LORD God proclaims. Whether they listen or whether they refuse, since they are a household of rebels, they will know that a prophet has been among them" (Ezekiel 2:4-5).

Speaking for God in conditions of exile often required standing up, confronting, and "care-fronting" the people of God about the truths of their devastating behavior and condition. Speaking the truth in love to worldly powers can be a difficult and awesome task. Such speaking demands not only physical action but also moral courage. Silence is nei-ther advised nor allowed when making prophetic utterances to those in exile. When it is time to speak, the prophet must speak because he or she represents not only the freedom and autonomy of God but also God's ines-timable love and concern for God's people.

How does one reconcile the language of judgment and condemnation contained in the prophetic oracles of proclamation with the language of hope and reconciliation that gets the people's attention, invites them to God, and heals their previous sins and wounds?

Live the Story

Do you ever lie awake at night, feeling alone and wondering how you could possibly be so isolated when surrounded by all the people you encounter every day? Do you suddenly start and shake during the late morning and realize you have been sitting lost in uncontrolled sadness because there is no one to understand the intricacies and mysteries of you? Have you more than once thought that you didn't fit well in your own skin and certainly not in society? Have you known a time (possibly even now) when you felt so far away from home that you wondered if you could ever get back there?

I write these questions now because we have been reading the story of Ezekiel, and it brings to mind the times I have felt alone and lost. It wasn't just when I was a teenager and was told that this was exactly what I should expect to feel. I don't think I was ever too young to experience isolation, though I didn't have the vocabulary to express it. Now that I am a senior, I sometimes seem to have made little progress in how I live my life.

Still, the feelings of exile, both personal and social, that we all feel in our alienation from God and each other do not have to become permanent states of being. Because of God's undying love for us, God ultimately desires redemption, restoration, and salvation. God often sends messengers to us who will lead us back home again if we are open to hearing the words and following the signposts. But heeding the messenger is not always easy. That word must break through years of human doubt encrusted by apathy; years of frustration driven by a lingering hopelessness that one's condition shall never improve.

That sense of home comes from rediscovering our place in the arms and hands of God first. It is realizing that we all belong to God. It means restoring a relationship of hope and confidence in God knowing that God is closer to us than we know. By finding our home in God again, we can sing the Lord's song in whatever strange and foreign places we find ourselves, personally and socially. This is the message of Ezekiel. This is God's primary purpose in the calling and commissioning of Ezekiel to a people alienated by their social and spiritual deportation.

A lesson for exiled persons today is that God is not limited to a geographical place; for in God's love, compassion, and justice, we discover God's purpose to reclaim the lost and to restore those who have been displaced in society and who cannot find their way home again. God is already present wherever we are. God will remind us of this reality by sending someone to meet us where we are to speak a message of redemption and salvation however far from home we may be carried.

We *can* go home again, and God sends a messenger who will point the way and lead us back home to God. Recall modern examples of groups of people who were virtually alienated and exiled from the larger society and the leaders called to lead the people back home. Here are some examples: Rosa Parks; Fannie Lou Hamer; Martin Luther King, Jr., giving birth to the Civil Rights Movement; Nelson Mandela in South Africa, called out of exile in prison to lead the South African people to freedom; Harriet Tubman, leading people out of slavery; Susan B. Anthony and the various leaders of the woman's suffrage and civil rights movements, leading the nation for women's right to vote; Betty Freidan and Gloria Steinem, leading the new movement for women's rights and freedoms. Today there are messengers of freedom, justice, and equality in the lesbian, gay, bisexual, and transgender community whose passion for justice under God is just as important as other movements for social change and freedom. There are even messengers still in Israel and Palestine who herald hope and freedom amid the challenging gridlocks of problems in the Middle East.

The prophets of old speak the hope for freedom and restoration to us, and prophets today remind us that God still awaits our return to God and to ourselves as the true community of love and faith in the journey of hope in this life.

In what ways has God commissioned you or others you know to stand and listen to and speak God's words of vision and hope to people in exile? Were you ever too afraid or too weak to stand amid such calling? What practical constraints did you face in accepting the challenge of such calling, and how did you overcome them? What words of comfort did you offer the exiles that gave them the courage to live faithfully to God amid seemingly hopeless conditions?

Recount if you can the numerous ways that the modern church is living in exile from the larger society. In what ways has the church helped create estrangement among its own members? How were these conditions overcome?

What experiences of exile do you see with members of your own faith community, and how have you helped create a climate of hope and an ethos of belonging for those who have been displaced?

How has the experience of your life and those of others who have been called to lead parallel Ezekiel's life?

What implications does the message of Ezekiel have for the practice of ministry today?

1. Willem A. VanGemeren, *Interpreting the Prophetic Word* (Grand Rapids, Michigan: Zondervan, 1990), 323.

2. Iain M. Duguid, *The NIV Application Commentary: Ezekiel* (Grand Rapids, Michigan: Zondervan, 1999), 35.

3. Ibid., paraphrase of words taken from "Exile and Dreams of Return," 48.

4. *The New Interpreter's Bible*, Volume VI (Nashville: Abingdon Press, 2001), 1081-1082.

5. Karl Barth, *The Word of God and the Word of Man* (Gloucester, Massachusetts: Peter Smith Publishers, 1978); Karl Barth, *The Humanity of God* (John Knox Press, 1960).

6. Richard P. Heitzenrater, *The Elusive Mr. Wesley*, Volume 2 (Nashville: Abingdon Press, 1984).

2.

"The Fire This Time!"

Ezekiel 4–24

Claim Your Story

I kept telling my seven-year-old daughter not to touch the hot stove while I was cooking. She promised that she would not play near the stove. She knew that she could get burned.

When preparing her breakfast one morning before school, she kept mischievously putting her hand near the stove and then suddenly snatching it back. I would shout, "Stop it!" She would begin snickering. "You think I'm playing?" I said. "If you keep putting your hand near that stove, one day you will get burned." After making her sit down at the kitchen table, the doorbell rang; I hurried from the kitchen to answer it. After receiving a package from the mail delivery driver, I suddenly heard a loud yelp from the kitchen, dropped the package, and ran back to find her holding her hand and whimpering in pain. When I asked what had happened, she reported that she had accidently let her hand touch the stove. I grabbed the first aid kit and began nursing her wounds while chiding her for being disobedient. "I have told you over and over not to get near the stove. Now Daddy has to put a salve on your burn so it can heal properly. Please don't touch that stove ever again," I said sternly.

So often this is our experience with God. God reminds us of the harmful consequences of our rebellious actions, but in defiance we must discover whether what God is saying is really true or not. In our rebellion, we touch the hot stove and get burned. Our sins do burn us; and while God can still provide a healing balm for those wounds caused by our sins, we often fail to obey God's warnings. The Israelites had to learn this lesson the hard way. After repeated promises to obey their covenant with God, their sins of rebellion caused them much pain. Something in them kept prompting them to touch the hot stove of sin and rebellion after repeated warnings by God not to do so.

Enter the Bible Story

A Sign for the House of Israel: Burn, Baby, Burn!

Ezekiel 4–5 tells the story of a people who have been "burned" by their sins and a God who burned in wrath against them.[1] They kept repeating their naughty and rebellious behavior and learned that their actions have consequences. Exile and the burning of Jerusalem were graphic reminders of how God's anger can burn against the people for their continued disobedience.

In Lesson 1 (Ezekiel 1–3), we discovered how the prophet was called and commissioned to awaken the people of God from the slumbers of exile and to provide a detailed message of how bad things really were for them. Jerusalem's neglectful decline and then devastation by Babylon became the visual sign of the people's spiritual and relational devastation. They had not kept God's commandments. They had surrendered their spiritual birthrights and had pandered after the false gods of their Babylonian conquerors. God was not pleased with their condition.

God asked the prophet to engage in a series of sign-acts[2] and perform some wild symbolic acts such as facing Jerusalem and taking a brick (4:1-3) "perhaps the size of one or two sheets of standard 8-1/2 x 11 paper"[3] and drawing a picture of Jerusalem on it, building a wall, setting up army camps and battering rams, taking an iron plate and setting up an iron wall between himself and the city (signifying the separation of God and God's people), lying on his left side for 390 days, and bearing the punishment of Israel one day for each year of their guilt and setting the guilt of the house of Israel on it (4:1-8).

Then God commanded Ezekiel to lie on his right side for forty days, to bear the guilt of the house of Judah. God bound Ezekiel with cords so that he could turn neither left nor right until he completed the days of his siege. God warned that God would destroy the food supply of Jerusalem and commanded the prophet to help the community visualize the shortages of food and water that would come (4:9-17).

Just as God's radical vision sounded the alarm and got Ezekiel's attention for his calling and commissioning for service, God used the prophet's acts to get the people's attention and rouse them out of their hopeless, detestable, and deplorable condition. Not only must they hear the word of God but see the word in action through the sometimes bizarre behavior of the prophet.

The prophet then shaved his head and beard and was commanded by God at the end of the siege to burn one third of his hair in the city, strike another third with the sword left and right, scatter one third to the wind, and then let loose the sword. From the final third, God asked the prophet to take a few strands and hide them in his garment and take another batch of hair and throw it into the fire to burn it up, saying that the whole fire will spread to the house of Israel (5:1-4).

God commanded the prophet to do some extraordinary and outlandish things to dramatize and interpret the extent of their folly as signs of God's complete displeasure because the people of Jerusalem rebelled against God's laws (5:5-17). God was furious with them. After all the years of covenantal promises, they still had not gotten it. They kept putting their hands on the hot stove of sin after God repeatedly warned them of the consequences, only to draw back in pain and disbelief when they were burned. In these judgment oracles or oracles of doom[4] (12:1–24:27), God started to really lay wrath on the people. God warned them of the future famines and plagues that would destroy them. Their burning sinful consumption and God's burning wrath continued.

God was very severe in condemnation of their sins and said that God will impose penalties they have never before experienced; for example, parents would eat their children and a third of the people would fall by the sword. God would show no compassion for them, shave them, shed no tears for them, and finally, scatter a third of them to the winds (5:8-13). God promised complete and consuming wrath on them. They would become a mockery and ridicule to the nations. God would release deadly arrows of famine on them, release wild animals on them, and leave them childless (5:14-17).

What images of devastation! God was completely fed up with the people, tired of their iniquity and refusal to heed divine commands and of their promises of devotional obedience while only showing rebellious waywardness. All appeals had been exhausted. The people had lost their way. No. They had lost their minds! God's patience had reached its limits. The heat of God's anger would only be surpassed symbolically by the effigies of God's people and all Jerusalem burning from their own sins.

The previous statements are component parts of Ezekiel's oracles of doom, followed by the continuation of blistering diatribes against the land itself and its unfaithful inhabitants (Chapter 6), and a description of the end that will follow (Chapter 7). The punishment for the people's sinfulness and rebellion against God was graphically explained. Ezekiel's second vision of the Temple was still filled with haunting imagery of Israel's devastation and further detail of Jerusalem's burning destruction (Chapters 8–11).

Backpacks for Exile
Ezekiel 12

Ezekiel had to provide another sign-act demonstration to the people because of their refusal to hear, see, and heed God. God had the prophet prepare and put on his "backpack" for going into exile, and then had him go into exile in the daytime and nighttime while the people watched. They watched, but they still did not see. When would they finally understand what God is trying to get them to do?

God asked the prophet to dig a hole through the wall and take his backpack through it while the people watched. Still, the people did not comprehend what the prophet was saying to them. They didn't even ask the prophet what he was doing in order to understand what the sign-acts meant for them. The sign-act of the backpack for exile in verses 1-16 was followed by the sign-act of fear and trembling in verses 17-20; and the people did not see the error of their ways or the exigencies of the devastations that awaited them.

The Foolish Prophets and Prophetesses Had Also "Burned" God's People With Their False Teachings and Deceptive Actions!

Ezekiel 13

The prophets, men and women, who had led the people astray, were also condemned. They were to be spokespersons for God, telling the people about the freedom, justice, and redemption of God. But their messages fell flat because they had not measured up to the living prophecies in their own lives. They had not walked the talk but were consumed with self-glorifying egotism.

They had been disobedient to God by idolizing themselves and performing worthless visions and deceptive divinations and were like "jackals among ruins" (verse 4), scavenging the dead carcasses of an exiled people, consigning their bones to the trash heaps of despair. They had not gone up to reinforce the wall of the house of Israel so that it would be ready to withstand the battle on the day of the Lord (verses 1-7).

The wall signified the strength and will of God to withstand the onslaught of the enemies of God. But the prophets lied about the Lord sending them to the people. They falsely claimed to speak for God, saying "peace" when there was no peace and saying that God was building a strong wall when in fact they laid cosmetic plaster on it. The plaster of self-righteousness that they used to reinforce the wall only weakened it. God sent rain and hail to weaken and tear down the wall because it was not constructed by the hands of the righteous but by the hands of the foolish. Every attempt to patch up their fallen relationship with God and plaster over the confidence of the people was only met with further disintegration among the people.

In truth, the prophets spoke only for themselves and consistently led the people astray. Their own sins of apathy and false leadership caused the people to continue to burn from the sins of rebellion. The people and Jerusalem lay in ruins because the leaders were useless and worthless and hapless. The false prophets helped bring ruin upon the people, and God was against them. God promised flooding rains and hailstones upon them. God would throw everything that he could against them. Divine anger still burned. God's mercy couldn't be quenched by their false overtures of devotion and obedience.

The prophetesses were not exempt either. They were prophesying from empty visions and their imaginations with their armbands and head veils to trap human lives while disguising their intentions (verses 17-23). The means and tools of their prophesying smacked of magic or even sorcery as suggested by the providential power of armbands and veils in leading the people afoul.

The armbands signified the ways in which the prophets "strapped" the people to themselves rather than lose the people for God, and the veils signified the covering of themselves so their sins might not be known. To break the spell of exile, the people were to be freed to worship, serve, return to, and honor God; but they were bound by the lure of symbols that signified their entrapment and bondage.

God would unbind the people from the snares of the prophetesses whose conniving interest was convincing the people to serve them rather than to serve God. Exile had become profitable because the prophets and prophetesses benefited from the spiritual and material exploitation of God's people. Instead of leading the people back to God, they instigated their woeful condition by perpetuating their spiritual displacement and dismemberment from the family of God.

The prophets and prophetesses of Israel were thus an impediment, a stumbling block, to the people's ability to hear and see the truth of Ezekiel's message. Their diversionary tactics led the people in futile directions that reinforced their hearing impairments and spiritual blindness. They became so accustomed to the false words of the foolish prophets that they were conditioned to not receive the truth of God as spoken to them by the prophet Ezekiel.

The Elders "Burned" the People With Their False Devotion
Ezekiel 4:1-11

We learned that part of the reason why the people are in exile in the first place is due to their lust for external idolatries and their tendency to chase the material and other seductions that led them astray. Had the people kept God's commandments, abided by the terms of their covenant with God, and not pursued the false idols and their allurements, they may

> **About the Christian Faith**
>
> ## Powerful Imagery of Fire
>
> The imagery of God's wrath symbolized by fire is less prominent in the New Testament. The notion of a God of retribution and restoration gives way to a God of forgiveness and salvation. Redemption and salvation are common elements in both covenants and ultimately demonstrate the desire of God in both the Jewish and Christian traditions to reestablish and renew solidarity and covenant within the faith communities.
>
> While images of God burning with anger and the people burning from their sins are less salient in the New Testament, fire is more prominently displayed as an expression of the cleansing and purifying power of the Holy Spirit. The people of God, burning with the fires of holiness, become vital forces for the transformation of themselves and the larger society by spreading the word of God (Isaiah 4:4-5; Matthew 3:11-12). The positive expressions of fire represent God's presence (Exodus 3:1-4; 13:21-22) and purify God's people (Isaiah 48:10; Malachi 3:3). The negative expressions of fire expressed God's wrath (Deuteronomy 32:22) and judged sinners on earth (Leviticus 10:2; Numbers 11:1-2).
>
> The tongues of fire expressed at Pentecost in the Holy Spirit (Acts 2:1-4) motivated the people into service for building the faith community. The tongues of flame spoken by the prophets were emblematic of some forms of prophetic speech that galvanized the faith community into remembrance of the promises of God and into communal reformation as the people of God. Fire is powerful imagery in the Old and New Covenant traditions.

have avoided exile altogether. With the elders, there was a continuation of a problem similar to the false and foolish prophets and prophetesses, which was the weakening of the people through idolatries.

Outwardly, the elders went through the motions of pretending to have absolute devotion to God. Inwardly, their hearts were elsewhere, which meant false devotion. The elders possibly had self-aggrandizing schemes that elevated them to privileged positions of leadership authority and power rather than truly devoting themselves to God. In fact, we might hazard to say that it was precisely this internal weakening of authority by leading the people astray with false devotion that induced the conditions leading to their susceptibility to captivity by the Babylonians in the first place.

History repeatedly reminds us that it is not only the enemies outside but also the enemies within that often cause the internal weakening of those forged bonds and strengths that prevent those strongholds of God from collapsing.

A Lesson From the Righteous Might Be a Good Place to Show the People How to Stop Being Burned by Their Leaders and Their Own Sins

Ezekiel 14:12-23

God provided the example of an unfaithful land that sinned against God and how God broke off its food supply, let famine destroy it, and eliminated both humans and animals. He lifted up Noah, Daniel, and Job as examples of people who deserved to be saved because they were righteous. Noah was righteous because he followed God's commands to build an ark to save humans and animals from the coming floods. Daniel was righteous because he remained true to his God even in captivity. Job was righteous because he did not forswear his allegiance to God even when his children and wealth were brutally taken away. God was giving the prophet hints of the kind of person who might qualify for exemptions from God's wrath and destruction. Noah got to work heeding God's warnings. Daniel kept his religion. Job kept the faith in the midst of personal hardships and catastrophes. The qualities exuded by these men are the characteristics that God hoped to see in the leaders and the people so that God might redeem and reclaim them. God asked Ezekiel to suppose that God would send sword, famine, wild animals, and plague. But even with all their righteousness, these three men would not have the power to save their sons and daughters or others in the land because that power was reserved for the one true sovereign God.

God reminded the prophet that even with the righteous present among the people in exile, it still would not be enough to save the land from ruin. With this hypothetical condition, God said to the prophet that if any righteous people could be found, the people of God would have a chance to move forward. If as few as three people who walk upright and serve the Lord could be found, there might be at least consolation among the surviving righteous.

Parables of Condemnation

Ezekiel 15–24

The Lord's word continued to be revealed to the prophet in the form of parables and metaphors that illustrated the sinful and detestable condition of the people. Israel was likened to images of the worthless vine and its wood that was consumed by fire (15:1-8); the faithless wife who prostituted herself for money and glory (16:1-63); the vine and the two eagles that threw away the fruit of its purposes by turning to things that would not promote its growth (17:1-24); the useless and sinful parents whose negative influences threatened the godliness, safety, and well-being of their children who were forced to make choices because of their lack of godly alternatives (18:1-32).

Condemnation of the people continued through parables of the two lion cubs (19:1-9), the uprooted vine (19:10-14), the two adulterous sisters (23:1-49), the useless cooking pot (24:1-14), and the death of Ezekiel's wife and the end of Jerusalem (24:15-27).

Live the Story

In these chapters, we have an exhaustive condemnation of the people for their sins. God's anger burns against them in their spiritual and communal lives. Yet throughout these chapters, we find hints of God's grace revealed in God's desire for a few righteous people to step up and stand out as living examples of those who might be spared from God's ensuing wrath. The fires of destruction burn the people, but God's burning love holds out the possibilities of redemption.

Often people just like us (and probably us too) act more like children than mature adults. We continually place our hands on the hot stove even when repeatedly warned against it. Where in your present experience have you observed signs of God's anger and burning against the people of God and the larger society? What struggles have you had with personal and communal sin that constituted rebellion against God? In what ways has God given you sign-acts as a way of revealing God's desire to rescue you from perishing? What has been your experience with the church's response to the sins of rebellion within the faith community? What was the ultimate outcome of such experiences? In what ways have you experienced the redemptive grace and mercy of God in the midst of your own sinfulness and how did God provide you with signs of that grace and redemption? As you think about these questions, consider how your personal experiences parallel those of both Ezekiel and the people who heard his prophecies. Also consider what changes you might want to make in your Christian journey.

1. The imagery of burning signifies the complete consumption of the people and Jerusalem caused by their sins. In Exodus 3 we find the imagery of the burning bush which is on fire "but didn't burn up." This image is both a symbol of God's holiness and God's desire to preserve and set free a people engulfed in flames of Egyptian slavery and oppression. The imagery of fires burning in Jerusalem and among the people in exile are those in which the people shall be consumed because they have lost reverence for God's holiness and have engaged in detestable practices that have profaned God's reality and presence in their lives. Ezekiel 15:1-8; 20:45-49 provide further depiction of fires raging and burning. The fires are also emblematic of God's anger that burns against them, and the complete devastation and consumption by sin.

2. Sign-acts are used by God to arouse the people into an awareness that God is trying to reach and transform them. Ezekiel almost theatrically demonstrates the extent to which God will go out of the way to get their attention and compel their return to God. Sign-acts are meant to provoke their attention and engage them in acts of positive change that will transform their woeful condition. God acts dramatically in human history. God must use a variety of methods to move the people from the slumbers of their continuing inertia often caused by sin and apathy to renewal and restoration.

3. Iain M. Duguid, *The NIV Application Commentary: Ezekiel* (Grand Rapids, Michigan: Zondervan, 1999), 88.

4. Judgment oracles or oracles of doom or oracles of bad news—these are the sacred writs of prophetic pronouncements. Words of warning from God flow through the prophet. They are words that make known the extent of the people's deplorable condition in the eyes of God, recounts in detail the nature of their sins, cites the causes of their apostasy, and describe the ultimate divine consequences of their actions.

3.

Let Neighboring Nations Beware!

Ezekiel 25–32

Claim Your Story

Do you remember the story at the beginning of Lesson 1 about the young siblings playing happily until they are no longer happy with each other? They suddenly found themselves in conflict, angry as can be, and then exiled from one another by Mom. Likewise, two school-aged friends worked cooperatively on a project until they disagreed. They no longer wanted to work together and stormed away.

Well, usually there is more to the story. The young siblings protest Mom's act of separation and loudly cry that she is unfair. They are best friends and don't want to be apart. When the school friends tell other friends about their disagreement and hurt feelings, someone affirms that the offending friend is rotten. This brings an immediate turnaround and a very sharp defense: "You can't talk about my best friend that way!"

We are all familiar with this phenomenon of conflict and support in close relationships. The understanding is that "I can wage war with my brother, sister, or friend; but you had best not say one single word of criticism about them." We have confidence riding in the back of our minds that soon all will be forgiven and then all will be well.

It is a similar story in Ezekiel. The Israelites have misbehaved and earned God's wrath. But that didn't mean that the neighboring communities could jump on them without God's intervention. Beware of an angry God!

Enter the Bible Story

God made God's desires known to the people of God through the words of the prophet Ezekiel. God ultimately wanted to reclaim and restore the people to a relationship where they honored God first and then abided by God's entreaties and commands. If they followed God's commandments and honored their covenant with God, their misery could be temporarily alleviated and then permanently eliminated. They would no longer be judged, condemned, and punished as exiles and could finally live the spiritually and materially rewarding lives that God meant for them to live. They stood between the brackets of Israelites chosen for God but condemned for their sins. God desired to reclaim them so that they again felt a sense of belonging in the family of God and no longer lived as exiles in a foreign land.

We saw in the previous lesson how the people of God continued to be burned for and by their sins. God was not amused. God's anger burned against them. To be sure, there were no easy answers and no easy exits from exile. As we have read, the people had to answer for their sins and own up to helping create their current plight. When they looked for the causes of their condition, they had to individually and collectively look in the mirror at themselves.

But there were others nearby who had to be reckoned with: The neighboring nations on their geographical borders who relished their demise. They were not innocent bystanders casting casual glances from afar; they celebrated with great joy at the downfall of Judah. Did they offer words of solace or consolation? Did they offer any entreaties to the God of Israel that would stave off God's wrath? Not that they could, but should they have? God didn't delight in the destruction of the people or the jeering of their enemies who mocked their devastation. God was against those who were against God's people and would bring judgment and destruction to them. All peoples and earthly powers are subject to God's power and are instruments in God's pursuit of divine justice.

Putting the Surrounding Nations on Notice: What Goes Around for the People of God Comes Around for the Enemies of God

God was not pleased at how the enemies of Judah made a laughing-stock of God's people and basked in the destruction of Judah and Jerusalem. The theme of judgment was also extended to them. The prophet Ezekiel, after giving exhausting criticism and denunciation through prophecies of doom against his own people, issued verdicts on those surrounding nations who had rejoiced gleefully in Judah's perishing, a demise from which the neighboring nations had hoped to handsomely profit.

God did not delight when others rejoiced at the misfortune of the beloved people by celebrating Israel's downfall. The gawkers and finger pointers, the haters and celebrators of the people's demise would eventually get their taste of God's wrath. In response to these insolent nations, God punished enemies of God for mocking and repudiating Israel's elect status.

The problem was not only the enemy *within*—those listless and languid spirits among their own people who gave up on God—but the *enemy without*, the external adversaries who delighted in the decimation and divisions of Israel's land and their failing relationship with God. Retributive justice followed to repay Judah's enemies lest they thought too highly of themselves, even more highly favored than God's people.

Just as God had no tolerance for Israel's internal reasons for collapse, God did not spare the external enemies and let the nations know that they too would experience their own forms of exilic displacement as had Israel and Judah in exile. These haughty nations would pay for their sins of insolence and boastfulness and their refusal to acknowledge Yahweh's sovereignty and majesty. What goes around for Judah likewise came around for the neighboring nations.

A member of my church tells the story of how her classmates had a party when she flunked biochemistry in medical school. They were jealous of her achievement of majoring in political science and passing the MCAT to enter medical school, and they ordered pizza and beer to celebrate her failure. The party lasted into the wee hours of the morning. The following words were posted on her apartment door the next day: "You think that you are better than us but you aren't. Welcome to our world. We are glad that you have gotten a taste of failure. Good luck on the repeat!" Signed, "Joyous, Thrilled, and Elated." Well, God was not joyous, thrilled, or elated.

God's judgment was aimed at four surrounding nations who were understood to have assisted Babylon in carrying out Israel's demise. Each of the nations had responses that were considered contemptible: Ammon to the east (25:3-7), Moab to the southeast (25:8-11), Edom to the south (25:12-14), and Philistia to the southwest (25:15-17).

About the Scripture

Oracles

Oracles are messages from God delivered through prophets. They are usually a response to a question, but not always. They are often associated with a certain location or precinct, but not always. Ezekiel carried the word of the God of the Israelites, but oracles were also associated with the gods of all the surrounding nations.

Some examples of oracles include:

1. Casting of lots (throwing of the *urim* and *thummin*, Exodus 28:29; 1 Samuel 14:41; 28:6; Acts 1:26) decided an action to be taken.
2. Dream oracles happened during sleep. Saul mentions such dreams when he attempts to get advice from Samuel before a battle (1 Samuel 28:7-25). Joseph's dreams in Matthew (1:20-21; 2:13, 19) are also examples.
3. Inspired oracles may have come as an answer to a question or may be unsought. They are often about salvation or judgment. They often predict suffering or healing.

The Contempt of Ammon

Ezekiel 25:1-7

God asked Ezekiel to dramatize his feelings toward the enemies of Israel by setting his face against the Ammonites and prophesying against them because they "clapped [their] hands and stamped [their] feet . . . with utter contempt for Israel's fertile land" (verse 6). Their sins were their cold disdain, their lack of sympathy for the people of God, and their refusal to help them at a critical time of need. Abraham Joshua Heschel says God's concern and the prophetic response are always rooted in a "religion of sympathy" to the people of God.[1] When the people were taken into exile, the Ammonites were smugly self-assured.[2] They saw the demise of Judah as a sure sign of their god's superiority over Yahweh. Walter Bruggemann speaks poignantly of the numbness and lack of compassion that accompanies systems of power in their treatment and social control of individuals. Antipathy instead of compassion is one of the many ways in which empire systems respond to the needs of the oppressed.[3]

There was a history of tensions between the two nations that was mostly in the form of territorial disputes and the manner in which the Ammonites not only allowed themselves to be used by the Babylonians against the people of Judah (2 Kings 24:1-2) but also united with Judah against the Babylonians (Jeremiah 27:3). The Ammonites were condemned because they mocked the destruction of the Jerusalem Temple, which had become a primary symbol of Israel's faith and its continuing relationship with God. Ammon viewed Israel as an adversary and scorned its relationship with Yahweh. In response to their gloating over Israel's demise, God promised that their land would be laid to waste, their food eaten, and their people destroyed (Ezekiel 25:6-7). Their contempt for Israel would translate into God's antipathy.

The Envy of Moab
Ezekiel 25:8-11

The old saying rings true—"Envy has a thousand eyes, none with correct vision." Like Ammon, Moab[4] evidenced ambivalent behavior toward Israel by assisting the Babylonians against Israel and then turning against Babylon by joining the anti-Babylonian coalition.[5] Moab's sin was its hypocritical self-righteousness, which condemned an adversary for weaknesses while aiding and abetting her enemies in its demise. It was mockery that said, *You are just like us. You are no better than us. All your claims of being elect and chosen of God ring hollow. Look at you. You have fallen like everyone else. Your claims to a sovereign and just God have no basis in reality. If your God is so great then why do you wallow in the quagmires of destruction like other nations? Both you and your God are worthless.* "The verdict on Moab was (verses 9-11) a manifestation of God's promise to curse those who curse Israel"[6] (Genesis 12:3). By cursing and insulting the people, they were cursing and insulting God.

God would open Moab's strongest and virtually invincible flank that was northwest of the city and expose it as an Achilles' heel to her enemies. Mountainous fortresses and strong cities that were once impregnable bastions of protection would now become the very pathways that their enemies use to subdue and vanquish them.[7] Moab would be decimated and her people "exiled" (Jeremiah 48:7-9). Neither Moab nor Ammon would be honored or remembered among the nations. Through its destruction, Moab would come to know the one true God of Israel. Envy can be a source of ill will, especially when it takes delight in the downfall of God's beloved people. The envy of Moab did not allow the people to see Judah or God clearly and compelled acts of retribution that precipitated their destruction.

The Enmity of Edom
Ezekiel 25:12-14

Edom went a step further than Ammon and Moab in its contempt for Judah by taking revenge on the house of Judah, which began as a conflict between Jacob (Israel) and Esau (Edom). The blood feud never ceased between them, and their mutual histories were filled with venomous retribution and recriminations. Edom's attitude of vengeance toward Israel culminated in the desire to possess Israel and Judah (Ezekiel 35:10) and became more appalling when it joined forces with Ammon and Moab to degrade Judah (36:5).

Of all Israel's foes, Edom should have known better. The rancor between the two nations went back to the theft of Esau's birthright. This act was never forgotten though the two brothers reconciled (Genesis 32–33). The most perilous form of their retribution occurred during the Babylonian siege of Jerusalem when the Edomites attacked the Jews in order to completely humiliate and destroy them; many people view these as criminal acts. The rivalry between the two brothers carried over into the way the nations treated each other. Edom's perpetual hatred of Israel would lead to its eventual destruction. Edom's downfall lay in active instigation of Israel's destruction.

The Hostility of Philistia

Ezekiel 25:15-17

Philistia's intent was to destroy Israel out of revenge. Chaim Herzog and Mordecai Gichon provide some information about the Philistine culture and lifestyle, writing that the Philistines "belonged to the family of 'Sea Peoples' that swept down the shores of the south-eastern Mediterranean in swift ships, with fire and sword. . . . Their mode of operation resembled that of the later Norsemen and Vikings. . . . The Philistines were master iron-smiths and provided their warriors with iron weapons, which the Israelites almost totally lacked."[8]

The two nations had a long and tenuous history evidenced with Sampson (Judges 13–16), Eli (1 Samuel 4), Saul (1 Samuel 13; 31), David (2 Samuel 5), Hezekiah (2 Kings 18:8), Jehoram (2 Chronicles 21:16-17), and Ahaz (2 Chronicles 28:18).[9] Because they enacted revenge with utter contempt and old hatreds, God threatened to overpower and obliterate them (Ezekiel 25:15-16). Philistia's history of hostility and vengeful attitudes and actions against Israel finally culminated in complete devastation of the Philistines.

Continuing Oracles of Condemnation Against Tyre

Ezekiel 26:1–28:19

The prophet continued his diatribes against Tyre, a major maritime economic and political power in the ancient world that escaped Babylonian aggression for a time. The prophet Jeremiah says Tyre joined Judah in revolt against Babylon (Jeremiah 27:3). Tyre was a powerful insular city shielded against normal strategies of land conquest, except when Alexander built an earthen corridor through the water to successfully attack the city by land. That opened the way for Nebuchadnezzar to lay siege to the city for thirteen years after his capture of Jerusalem.[10]

Tyre "laughed at" Jerusalem (Ezekiel 26:2) and wanted to seize its spoils. Ezekiel shared his lament for the city and shared a eulogy for its death. The successive waves of conquest by Persians and Romans and then Saracens in the fourteenth century hastened the city's dissolution.[11] Even a maritime power, a fortified city, and a bulwark of impregnability against its foes, Tyre was no match for the God of Israel.

Against Sidon
Ezekiel 28:20-26

Ezekiel then told of God's condemnation of Sidon for its contempt of Israel by prophesying God's curse of plague and brandishing of a bloody

About the Christian Faith
Finding Common Ground

We have all seen how perceptions that individuals and groups have of one another can skew their relationships. This is true even in the Christian community, which often has a limited understanding of Judaism and its spiritual parentage of Christianity. Christianity and Judaism come from the same spiritual roots, but often the people live with enmity and hostility toward each other. In many respects, Jews and Christians now live almost as exiles from each other. This is curious given the fact that Judaism is the spiritual source of Christianity. The same can be said of members of the Jewish faith, whose wounds and pain from the anti-Jewish sentiments fostered by segments of the Christian church still leave memories of estrangement, suspicion, and division among Jews and Christians.

Both communities must make a more concerted effort in building bridges of hope and understanding between the two communities. We have done this at Hope United Methodist Church by sharing Seder meals with various Jewish synagogues and hosting peace forums on the Middle East. It makes no sense for communities who are so close in faith, religious history, and traditions to remain so far from one another. We must all work to ensure that we are no longer living estranged from one another and begin dialogue that will enable us to see the things that we have in common as communities of faith.

The same can be said of other religious faiths and communities such as Muslims, Sikhs, Hindus, and others. We should work to find our common ground as faith communities rather than standing in judgment of respective belief systems of which we know little or nothing. We can help each other in times of need and begin building bridges that will thwart any feelings of exile from each other. God wants to restore us all to our rightful place of heritage and promise as people of God.

sword. But in this oracle, God's judgment was for good because Yahweh would be glorified among the Sidonians who would realize that God was truly the Lord and God (verse 22). As a result, the house of Israel would no longer suffer from neighbors holding it in contempt.

A Glimpse of Restoration
Ezekiel 28:25-26

Here we read glimpses of restoration and relief. God demonstrated holiness and sovereignty. God cast a vision of restored people. They lived safely on fertile land and planted vineyards and built houses. And when God executed judgment on those who held God's people in contempt, they would know the Lord as their God.

Against Egypt
Ezekiel 29–32

Egypt was condemned for Pharaoh's imperial claims that the Nile was his and not God's creation (verses 8-12) and for Egypt's failure to help Israel when it attempted to relieve Jerusalem from the Babylonian siege in 588 B.C.[12] Egypt's dilemma was in its earthly claims of divine authority; its pomp, arrogance, and pride; and its imperial claims boasting power greater than the God of Israel. Its political superiority, power, and invincibility would become symbols of humanity's inherent corruption and its constant attempts to bring down the people of God.

The problem of exalting earthly leaders above God was an issue in the Exodus of the Israelites from Egypt and a later fissure between the Jews and the Roman line of Caesarian rulers and conquerors, extending to the time of Christ. Humanity's worldly empire versus God's kingdom on earth was a continuing theme of conflict in the oracles against Egypt.

Live the Story

In this lesson, we read how the prophet Ezekiel was tasked with pronouncing oracles against those neighboring nations harboring contempt for Judah and disdain for Yahweh. While the geopolitical implications of the oracles can be evidenced, they also contain ideological and theological components. God was angered by Judah's state of exile and enraged by the manner in which its neighbors kicked it while it was down. While God's anger with Judah's enemies brought no real satisfaction for a people suffering the woes of exile, it reminded its adversaries that they were fair game too.

How often in our faith journey have we seen this story repeated? People who are able to lend a helping hand to neighbors in need turn the other way. We see this among groups of people, and we see it individually among persons who consider themselves good neighbors. We are reluctant to lend a helping hand to those we believe are already more advantaged than many others.

I recall an experience in my ministry where members of the same faith community would not stretch themselves to help other members in need because they were jealous of the material wealth of those persons. The question that was posed to me is one that I will never forget: "Why should we help them? They already have everything that they need. In fact, they have more than us."

Although Judah's situation was somewhat different, there was a perception that as the chosen people they had all the blessings they needed and whatever misfortune they experienced was brought upon themselves. Too often jealousy, apathy, and enmity create barriers between individuals and communities. What we need is compassion, a fervent eagerness to help others despite their social or economic condition because it is the morally right action and the very thing that God expects of us. The superficial barriers that human beings create among themselves in order to distinguish themselves should be laid down and made into bridges of hope, understanding, and mutuality among persons. The Israelites' experience of exile was made worse by their surrounding neighbors' antipathy toward them.

Have you ever experienced a form of exile in your relationship with God, self, family members, or the larger faith community? If yes, please describe.

In what ways does your own personal experience with estrangement or exile parallel the experience of Judah?

Describe instances in which you have encountered envy, enmity, and hostility in your experience of exile. How did these negative expressions toward you compound your situation?

Describe instances in which your behavior toward a person or persons led them to feel alienated, estranged, and exiled in your community.

What other instances can you cite when you have seen similar dynamics of exile and estrangement played out among persons?

When have you found yourself in the role of a prophet who must speak biting truths to the people of your own faith community or congregation?

In what ways has your own faith community exemplified exilic patterns of existence? How did you become aware of them and implement positive change in response to them?

1. Abraham Joshua Heschel, *The Prophets* (Peabody, Massachusetts: Hendrikson Publishers, 2004), 87-103. "In contrast to . . . a *homo apathetikos*, the prophet may be characterized as a *homo sympathetikos*." Although God becomes angry with the people for their sinful failings, God ultimately sympathizes with them. The prophet becomes the messenger who reminds the people that God ultimately cares for them. However harsh and caustic God's words to them, God ultimately desires their return to him.

2. *The Expositor's Bible Commentary*, Volume 6, Frank Gaebelein, ed. (Grand Rapids, Michigan: Zondervan, 1986), 865. "The Ammonites descended from Lot's incestuous relationship with his youngest daughter (Gen 19:30-38). They settled in the Transjordan area south of Gilead, around their later capital Rabbah."

3. Walter Bruggemann, *The Prophetic Imagination*, Second Edition (Minneapolis, Minnesota: Augsburg Fortress Press, 2001), 28-43.

4. *The Expositor's Bible Commentary*, 866. "The Moabites descended from Lot's incestuous union with his eldest daughter (Gen 19:30-38). They normally inhabited the area on the Transjordan plateau between Wadi Arnon on the north and Wadi Zered on the south, though they often pushed north of Wadi Arnon."

5. See the study columns on Ammon, Moab, Edom, and Philistia in Marvin A. Sweeney, "The Book of Ezekiel" in *The Jewish Study Bible*, Adele Berlin and Marc Zvi Brettler, eds. (New York: Oxford University Press, 2004), 1089-1091.

6. *The Expositor's Bible Commentary*, 866.

7. *The Jewish Study Bible*, 1090-1091. See the study columns on Ammon, Moab, Edom, and Philistia.

8. Chaim Herzog and Mordechai Gichon, *Battles of the Bible: A Military History of Ancient Israel*, reprint (Indiana: Greenhill Books/Lionel Leventhal, Limited, 2006), 80-81; also see *The Expositor's Bible Commentary*, 868.

9. *The Expositor's Bible Commentary*, 868. Also see the study columns on Ammon, Moab, Edom, and Philistia in Marvin A. Sweeney, "The Book of Ezekiel" in *The Jewish Study Bible*, 1089-1091; and Herzog and Gichon, 80-81.

10. *The Expositor's Bible Commentary*, 869-885.

11. Ibid.

12. Ibid., 888-905.

4.

"I Want You Back!"

Ezekiel 33–48

Claim Your Story

Two of my favorite songs are Simon and Garfunkel's "Bridge Over Troubled Water" and Marvin Gaye's "What's Going On?" The lyrics of the first song begin with weariness and feeling small. Eyes are filled with tears. Times are rough, and you feel friendless. How often in life do we face these conditions? This song was especially appealing to the college students who listened to it on the radio or cassettes and later 8-track tapes when it was released in 1970. The song gathered together all the personal fears of living in the present and doubts about the future. Paul Simon's lyrics accurately described the feeling of being down and out. Marvin Gaye's song became the anthem of a generation that questioned war and the various forms of social alienation in American society.

These two songs, among many other tunes of that era, captured the angst of young people. It was the mood of an American culture in upset and turmoil. Young men were shipped off to distant Southeast Asia where life was strange and terrifying because war was all they would experience. The Civil Rights Movement gained prominence with people marching for their rights and protesting centuries of racial oppression. Death was around every corner, and their loved ones shared the terror with them. A nation asked itself, *What's going on? What are we doing? Why are we there? Are we doing the right thing? Can this be God's will for us? Where is God when we call? What did we do to earn this torture?* Perhaps those who lived during this time can understand what Israel felt in exile. "Bridge Over Troubled Water," for all its pathos, offers words of hope. Someone is present to support you. You will be comforted. A new time has come, a time to shine. Your dreams of peace will be granted.

Ezekiel was like a bridge over troubled water telling the people what God was going to do to restore their lives.

Enter the Bible Story

The days of weariness in exile seemed to be finally coming to an end. After all that the people did to rupture relations with God and invoke God's wrath, God's love appeared as new radiant light engrossing the people of God in the warmth of its glow. The new light at the end of the tunnel was not the light of an oncoming train, but the light of God, resplendently breaking forth with new hopes and possibilities for new life. But there was still some unfinished business. The enemies of God sacked the Temple at Jerusalem, the place where God exclusively dwelt, and the great city fell. The words of the prophet heralded this dismal state of affairs. Both the city and the Temple were in ruins; all would be restored eventually but not the same as it was before.

After all that, God did a new thing. It was time for the repentance of the people, the return of the people to God, and the return of Yahweh to the Temple in Jerusalem.[1] Jerusalem had fallen. God had not forgotten the wickedness of the people and the ways in which their leaders—including the prophets, prophetesses, and the shepherds—led them astray. However, the sovereign God who desired to restore righteousness among the people and holiness to God's name had the final say in all the earthly affairs of Israel. Justice was restored and righteousness once again reigned.

Closing the Gap

Through the prophet, God worked to bridge the gap between God and the people of God. God initiated this closing by sending the prophet to the people; and the prophet stood in the gap with his message of judgment, hope, and restoration. Ezekiel was bridging the awareness between how they had fallen away from God and how God was reclaiming them and returning to them. There were still chasms between their former disbelief and their new belief in God. They saw how God worked to restore them from their condition of exile. The theme of divine judgment in the previous chapters turned to the restoration of God's people to their land and covenant. God promised to make an airtight relationship with the people. God promised to remove all present gaps in their faith that prevented them from truly seeing God at work in new ways in their lives. God no longer allowed their leaders to create gaps in knowledge, faith, and remembrance of Yahweh by making false promises and leading the people astray. God took the remains and ruins of their present condition and rebuilt the house of Israel with all the majesty, splendor, and power that Yahweh commanded. The people no longer pursued the worship of idols or engaged in detestable practices that dishonored God's name and brought themselves ruin.

Despite the ravages of personal apostasy and divine retribution for ungodliness and unfaithfulness, the oracles against Judah (Chapters 1–24), and the oracles against the foreign nations (Chapters 25–32), God finally revealed the purpose of these actions by telling and showing the people that he wanted them back. God sought their return. God sought to help the people understand that they would finally know God and bring honor back to the Holy Name. In the end, there is good news (Chapters 34–48).

The prophet Ezekiel, as watchman and lookout for the people, had to set a different tone to his messages. The mood of Ezekiel shifted from diatribes of despondency to praise reports of new life by divine restoration. He helped a besieged and beleaguered people grasp a new and more glorious vision of God, one filled with the hope and promise of divine possibilities amid their own hopeless disabilities. After years of turning their sights away from God in sorrow and disillusionment before and during their exile, God made the watchman responsible for the people. If he did not warn the people and thus allow them to be taken further away in sin, God would hold him responsible for their blood (33:6). The prophet and the people had come too far in their miserable journey to turn back now.

The watchman who lived among his people had to follow through with the message until the end. He echoed their despondency and defeatism. They became aware of how they had come to this condition and of their personal role in their own demise, the ruin of Jerusalem, and the destruction of the Temple (33:10). The prophet said, "Turn, completely turn from your wicked ways! Why should you die, house of Israel?" (33:11). A special invitation came to the people by way of the prophet, by that time a proven faithful watchman who had done his duty. The restoration of the people of God would be complete and exhaustive. No segment of their personal and communal life went untouched. God had a master plan for their renewal.

Good News! A Good Shepherd Shall Lead Them. The People, the Land, and Their God Returned and Restored

Ezekiel 34

The prophet's work to call and bring the people out of exile and back to God was done as a good shepherd leads his or her flock. Instead of the shepherd forcing a rule of injustice upon the people, God gathered the people as a good shepherd does and provided them with all the necessities of their complete restoration. God set into motion a new paradigm or model of pastoral leadership. They no longer wandered as stray sheep. Wild animals no longer attacked them. They were no longer in need of fresh rains and fertile land. They "grazed" freely on good land and were delivered from the yoke of their masters. They no longer experienced famine or were disgraced by other nations. They were safe. God bridged the gap between God and the people by the crook and compassion of the shepherd. God was their shepherd, giving them the comfort, safety, and protection they needed for their full feeding, redemption, and restoration. The people of God would finally know that it was God who rescued them after their scattering among the nations. They knew it was God who came for them to bring them back as a flock into the fold. By following the shepherd and rejoining the fold, the people knew that God was with them and would not forsake them. Their future was permanently in the hands of the good and faithful shepherd.

About the Scripture

Of Sheep and Shepherds

Note that the shepherd always goes after the lost sheep (Matthew 10:5-6). The image of the good shepherd is the ultimate symbol of God's comfort, care, and restoration. As a good shepherd searches after wayward sheep, God seeks the people who have gone astray. As a good shepherd holds those sheep whose legs have been broken, God holds the people in God's arms and nurses them back to health. "Sheep are built in such a way that if they fall over on their side and then onto their back, it is very difficult for them to get up again. They flail their legs in the air, bleat, and cry. After a few hours on their backs, gas begins to collect in their stomachs, the stomach hardens, the air passage is cut off, and the sheep will eventually suffocate. This is referred to as a 'cast down' position.

"When a shepherd restores a cast down sheep, he reassures it, massages its legs to restore circulation, gently turns the sheep over, lifts it up, and holds it so it can regain its equilibrium."[2]

Sheep do not follow the old axiom that there is strength in numbers. The flock's large population does not guarantee protection from their predators. They need a good shepherd, someone to guide and care for them and lead them safely home again. God, the good shepherd, will lead the people back to him and their journey will not be filled with the hazards and problems that initially led them astray.

The Mountains and Cities Restored

Ezekiel 36:1-15

God gathered the Israelites as a shepherd gathers his own sheep for care and safekeeping. God not only cared about the people; he also cared for the land. Even the mountains and cities spoke of the coming glory of God. In their conquest of God's people, the enemies of Israel and Judah insulted the land and trounced all the good earth. The Promised Land of God was filled with the splendor of luscious landscapes, but the surrounding nations ravaged the land to make it an object of slander and derision. The land was a gift and a promise made possible by God's generosity.[3]

The land that was formerly rich and fertile with blooming trees and freshwater streams became barren and suffered from ungodly insults and intrusions of foreign conquerors, defiling Israel's purity and cleanliness and leaving its cities and valleys in ruins. The scorched-earth policies of their enemies made a mockery of God and creation.

The prophet reminded them that they would no longer suffer ridicule and debasement. God would cause the trees of Israel to bear fruit, waters to run fresh, and seeds to be sown that would once again bring great harvests. The land, people, and animals would multiply and replenish. The whole house of Israel would be restored. The people would walk openly and freely through the land of God. The people would once again lay claim to their inheritance and would never again be deprived of their inheritance!

The People Restored With a New Heart and Spirit

Ezekiel 36:16-38

The true reasons for the people's original dispersal among other nations are cited. The people defiled the land. They degraded God's name and defiled themselves with idols. God did this new thing to inspire the people to understand God's goodness and holiness and God's desire to restore God's good name. God did this fresh thing for himself so that they understood that God knew the extent of their falling away and how they caused their condition. "I will make my great name holy, which was degraded among the nations when you dishonored it among them" (verse 23).

The prophet told the people that when God made God's name holy, he gathered them from all countries and brought them back to their own fertile land. God sprinkled clean water on them, cleansed them of all pollution, and put a new heart and spirit in them so the people would know that the sovereign and powerful Yahweh was the only true God. Then the people would walk according to God's regulations and carefully observe all God's laws (verses 23b-28).

God reached into the people's hearts so that they knew the full intent of Yahweh, which was to reclaim them as their God, restore them as God's people, and renew them with a fresh, resilient, and obedient spirit that would not cause them to languish in the apostasies and idolatries of their earthly hosts. God reconditioned the people to have hearts of obedience, loyalty, and trust instead of rebellion; a heart of service and humility; a heart that felt others' pain and turned to God as a source of hope and healing. The people had a new spirit for God, a spirit of hope and liberation, peace, and spiritual prosperity; a spirit that did not cower to the false gods or submit to their false promises; a spirit that allowed them to once again know that God is their God and they are God's people.

Their restoration was complete both externally and internally. God gathered them unto himself, reclaimed them, and protected them as a good shepherd his sheep. God restored the land and renewed it from the ravages of Israel's personal abuse by indifference and its misuse by foreign invaders whose geographical conquest and annexation made the land more desolate. God renewed the people with a right heart and spirit. With mind, body, heart, and soul, they became the people they were called to be in the name of Yahweh. Their restoration was complete inside, outside, in nature, and on land. Everywhere, signs of return were manifested in the symbols of religious faith. It touched every aspect of their lives in Yahweh, personally, socially, spiritually, and materially.

Yes! These Dry Brittle Bones Can Live!
Ezekiel 37:1-14

The valley of dry bones was the site of an ancient battle where bleached bones became the ultimate symbol of the people's spiritual inertia and physical depletion. They were dead spiritually, emotionally, and mentally. Every image symbolizing the vitality and faith of the people of God was juxtaposed to the imagery of death. While the amenities and opportunities of total assimilation into Babylonian culture were all around them, they became physically anesthetized and spiritually enfeebled by the experience of exile. The bones were a symbol of their complete devastation and bodily separation as a faith community.

The separated bones lay in the valley where escape seemed impossible. They were without life, even the possibility of life. The body became a metaphor for an aggregate Israel, the faith community, signifying those life-sustaining essentials that made all movement and life possible. Without living bones, the body cannot have life. Restoration must first be skeletal, including the renewing of spine and vertebrae as the basic supporting structure of life, which the body depends on for movement.

God asked the prophet whether the bones could live again (verse 3). The prophet says that God knew the answer and then God asked the prophet to tell the bones that God will breathe new life into them so the bones could live again. Breath is the indispensable element of life. *Breath* is translated as *ruach* (Hebrew) and *pneuma* (Greek). Once the prophet prophesied the breath from the four winds into the bones, they came to life and lived again! It was the holy breath of God breathed into the dead bones that brought them back to life. It was the very breath of Yahweh breathed into a dead and lifeless people that ensured their revival and restoration.

Life had been restored. The house of Israel lived again. The people came forth from their graves and all the land reverberated with vitality. With new breath and new life, the people once again knew that Yahweh was their God and they were his people.

The People and Kingdoms No Longer Divided
Ezekiel 37:15-28

Now that the dead bones were revived with new breath from God, the kingdoms of Judah and Israel are finally united. God told Ezekiel to perform another sign-act by taking two separate sticks and then join them into one stick. One of the sticks was carved to represent Joseph, associated with Ephraim. The other was carved with an inscription representing Judah (verses 15-17). The symbolism of fusing two sticks into one stick represented the power of God to unite the Israelite nations despite the divisions that caused their exile and fragmentation. The people of Israel have been divided and conquered by others because they were not united in their purpose as God's chosen people.

The reasons for the initial rift between the nations would finally end. The Israelites were united under King David, one shepherd to protect and lead God's people in the ways of God, one covenant of peace forever, and one eternal sanctuary among them (verses 24-28). The scandalous succession of corrupt leaders sponsoring the spiritual demise of God's people had been a large part of their problem. They had fallen away in part because their leaders had fallen away. The renewed people would no longer tarnish and pollute themselves with the idolatrous corruptions of their adversaries. They were to be purified and cleansed from the defilements of exile, making way for their complete restoration. And the resulting blessings shall flow unhindered for generations to come. The nations will know that Yahweh was God. The people would know that Yahweh was their God and that they once again were God's people.

Even With the Rise of Gog, the People's Eternal Security Will Not Be Threatened

Ezekiel 38–39

In their state of restoration, the people were not threatened. "No weapon fashioned against you will succeed" (Isaiah 54:17). God permitted the rise of Gog to test the people's assurance and safety in God. The only reason Gog was allowed to rise against the newly restored people was so that God could demonstrate and flex spiritual muscles by defeating any enemy that came their way. The people will then finally know that God really meant business. All previous talk of restoration and redemption was finally fulfilled in the vanquishing of Gog and his final defeat and disposal.

Now, a New Vision: The Temple Restored!

Ezekiel 40–48

In the twenty-fifth year of exile, on the tenth day of the month, fourteen years after Jerusalem was struck down, Ezekiel received a new vision of Israel's return and restoration (Ezekiel 40:1). Everything will take its rightful place in the new arrangement. With revival and restoration comes the renewing of the Temple and the holy city Jerusalem. During a time when religious monuments were a symbol of God's continuing favor and prosperity among the people, the new vision heralds a final restoration of Israel's most sacred shrine.

The prophet's vision spared no detail. There were gates, rooms, altars, tables, chambers, sanctuary, courtyards, windows, porches, steps, and archways. There were two prominent purposes for the new Temple. The

Temple was to provide a throne for God among the people in all of God's resident glory (43:6-7). Second, the Temple complex reflected God's holiness by its walls of separation, various courts, and temple divisions (40:5; 42:1-12). Worship was free and unhindered, and the overall design reminded the people of their former iniquities.[4] The East Gate was most prominent among all the gates. Ezekiel provided a meticulous description of the Temple in all of its magnificence in Chapters 40–48.

The Temple as a perfect physical reconstruction was symbolic of the perfect power of God in consummating the return, restoration, and renewal of the people. God spared no detail in exacting the right "measurements" (breadths, heights, and widths) of this new restorative relationship. The new Temple, which was as sprawling and majestic as a new city, became a living monument to the glory of God and the renewal of God's people for all time.

The New Role of Priests and Princes

Ezekiel 44–45

The priests did not indulge in the practices that initially led the people of Israel astray from God. They were a big cause of the people's falling away from God in the first place. Had they kept the duties and ordinances and continually consecrated and not desecrated themselves in the eyes of God, the people might have avoided their subsequent separation and exile.

In their renewed role of modeling the spiritual restoration of God's people, they were ministers in God's sanctuary and gatekeepers of God's house who shall teach God's people the difference between holy and the ordinary and cause them to discern between clean and unclean. The priests will execute judgments according to God's laws in cases of civil conflict, observe instructions and regulations regarding God's festivals, and keep the Sabbath holy (44:15-31). The princes will cease their oppression of the people, stop their evictions, and establish justice and righteousness among the people (45:9-10).

Keeping the Sabbath, Festivals, and Offerings: The Just
Redistribution of Land Among the Tribes

Ezekiel 46–48

The restoration of God's people also means restoring the ritual ordinances of priests, worship observances, and caretaking of the Temple. While some ritual observances are equivalent to the Mosaic worship prescriptions, they are not exactly the same because the people themselves have been renewed and restored. Worship is done so that justice and righteousness shall ultimately prevail throughout the land. The fresh vital spirit that the people of God bring to worship and the celebration of their return breathes new life into Temple practices. No longer led astray by the defilements of corrupt priests and worldly princes and no longer enmeshed in a

---

About the Scripture

Prophetic Speech

God does want the people of God to return and sends messengers to explain their condition and how they got there. The messengers also remind the people of God's desire for their return and what that means for the future. We read this promise and this hope in the words of Isaiah, Jeremiah, and Ezekiel. The various forms of prophetic speech contain various formulas for announcing God's vision and hope for the people.

Most forms of prophetic speech contain elements of harsh criticism of the people and the sins they have manifested in creating their present condition. In the prophetic books of the Bible, such criticism usually contains graphic imagery that renounces impudent behavior and issues a series of warnings that portend the people's final decimation. Such language and speech causes discomfort, resistance, and resentment among the people. The fate of Jeremiah and of Jesus, the apostles, and Paul in the early Jesus movement all attest to the violent consequences of prophetic speech when directed at the people of God and to kings in power.

The harsher oracles of speech emblematic of the prophets in the former covenant are toned down somewhat in the New Testament except during the various skirmishes of Jesus with the Shammai School of Pharisees versus the Hillel School and in the subsequent work of the apostles during the later time of persecution.[5]

In looking at the various forms of prophetic speech in the former and present covenants, we see similarities and differences in tone, character, quality, and gravity of prophetic discourse. The ultimate result of such speech, however, is the positive transformation of the people of God, a conversion that ultimately leads to their return and restoration as God's people.

spirit of idolatry and rebellion, the people of God have a new sense of the glory of Yahweh's presence and their worship now has permanent value and meaning.

The justice and mercy of God is revealed in the just redistribution of land among the eleven tribes (Levi is landless). God dwells at the center of the place called "The LORD Is There" (48:35).

Live the Story

Thousands of years after Ezekiel revealed God's messages to God's people, we have come together to study God's Word and to hear what God expects of us. We sometimes pay attention to and obey God's will, but other times we ignore God's clear word for us.

Contrasting ourselves with the Israelites, we have different names, different settings, and different cultures; but the stories of the interactions between humans and God remain essentially the same. From the time we are small children, we believe we know how to live our lives. Though we have loving parents and wise teachers, we learn the word *no* early and use it often. Many of us have been in Sunday school all our lives and have heard the Bible stories over and over again. Still, we model disobedience more often than we live God's way.

We are hardly more obedient as we reach adulthood and our mature years. In fact, calling them "mature" carries a high degree of irony. We pay a heavy price for our disobedience, making life more difficult at every step. But every step is another opportunity to listen to God and choose God's way. Every step is a chance to take the bridge over troubled water and find the life-giving waters promised by the prophets. Every step takes us closer to God's vision for all of creation. Every step leads to God.

As you survey the account of Ezekiel's call to the people to turn back to God and behold God's ultimate plan of return and restoration from the experience of exile, what parallel lessons can you draw in your personal experience?

God's judgment precedes exile, and exile is followed by restoration; but renewal does not come without a price. What price did the people of God ultimately pay in their exile?

Where do you see signs of exile and restoration in the faith community, for example, the church and its leadership today?

How do you foresee the return of God's people in a society that is increasingly materialistic and the love of power and the allegiances between religion and the state seem to overwhelm the sense of divine purpose?

What is the ultimate message of the Book of Ezekiel? How can this message of hope help people still living in exile today?

What would you say to people as they seek to understand their situation in the present world?

1. Walter Bruggemann, *Out of Babylon* (Nashville: Abingdon Press, 2010), 96-97.

2. *Our Daily Bread Devotional Bible*, Second Edition (Discovery House Publishers, 2012), 592.

3. Walter Bruggemann, *The Land: Place of Gift, Promise, and Challenge in Biblical Faith* (Minneapolis, Minnesota: Augsburg Fortress Press, 2002).

4. *The Expositor's Bible Commentary*, Volume 6, Frank Gaebelein, ed. (Grand Rapids, Michigan: Zondervan, 1986), 946-947.

5. Dr. Ron Moseley, *Yeshua: A Guide to the Real Jesus and the Original Church* (Clarksville, Maryland: Messianic Jewish Publishers, 1996), 107-108.

5.

From the Outside Looking In to the Inside Looking Out: You've Got to Serve Somebody!

Daniel 1–6

Claim Your Story

Faith is always lived out under specific social and environmental conditions. It does not thrive in a vacuum nor can it be dispensed like salt from a shaker. Its value lies in its internal strength and its capacity to help persons adapt to external circumstances while adopting firm resolution to press on toward the prize.

Think of the times in your life when you were on the outside of important events rather than on the inside. Perhaps you wanted badly to make a contribution to the team but couldn't because of some limitation. Some experiences in life find us on the outside of events, almost powerless to influence events on the inside of the "arena." That is exactly how my son felt after tearing his ACL in the football preseason. The rehabilitation process was long and challenging and required many weeks of going to physical therapy after school three times a week. When baseball season rolled around the following April, he could not practice or play with the team because his healing time extended until the end of May. He still suited up for each game and played a supportive role for his teammates that season. One day he said, "Dad, I feel isolated sometimes, riding the bench all alone."

Rather than letting him lament his condition by pouting himself into despondency and negatively affecting the morale of his teammates, I told him to be hopeful, to be eager and ready to help the team when called to play. It took time for his physical injury and emotional wounds to heal. Finally, near the end of the season, his number was called; and he stepped up and helped the team win games. His feelings of "exile" for being sidelined due to injuries did not ultimately dampen his spirit. He did everything he could to help the team, even when his number was called later than he expected. He cheered the team and rallied them from the dugout of his own feelings of restriction and "captivity" despite his own personal trials.

Perhaps this is similar to the experience of Daniel, who felt sidelined from participating with his home team after being deported to Babylon. However, he soon found his true place when called upon to help Team Judah. The external demands of captivity did not deter his work in helping his countrymen find their gifts and graces in a foreign land. Whatever circumstances in which we find ourselves, we can make a positive difference. We can draw from an interior faith and strength that will allow us to ride out the storms of our individual circumstances and help those around us to know the power and truth of a living faith.

Enter the Bible Story

A True and Living Faith

King Nebuchadnezzar of the neo-Babylonian Empire exiled Daniel and his three companions Hananiah (Shadrach), Mishael (Meshach), and Azariah (Abednego). Throughout this story, we see how Daniel and the three men held God's favor by their heroic obedience and steadfast faith in Yahweh. While training courtiers in "languages, court protocol, and international relations was common in the ancient world,"[1] the narrative reveals the trainees were not completely compliant with the king's wishes and demands. They changed their geographical position but not their spiritual dispositions; they remained true to their God.

As the exiled Daniel ascended the ranks of leadership in Babylon, it became clear that human power is no match for God's power. Daniel's extraordinary ability to decipher the king's dreams and foretell the future and his determination to hold on to his faith at all costs—even while in service to his "superiors"—made him an exceptional example of the power and sovereignty of faith.

Exile essentially meant being on the outside, estranged from self, God, and community, and living externally to those events and circumstances that controlled one's destiny. Exile is dislocation from those familiar places that we have called home. While Daniel's new home was the Empire of Babylon, he was *in* but not *of* that empire. Transplanted to this new land, Daniel maintained his personal faith and integrity. He used his spiritual and intellectual gifts to speak God's truth to those in power.

Physical exile need not equate spiritual, relational, or psychological exile—a permanent dislocation from one's true self and the one true God. It also need not mean a diminished capacity to use one's services in the employ of masters. It means finding those still points where we live within the tensions of faith and freedom, the demands of captivity and the quest for autonomy, the need for creative self-expression and the realities of absolute conformity. Singer and social commentator Bob Dylan's song says, You've "gotta serve somebody." Wherever we are, we must find ways of using our gifts to improve our lives and the lives of those around us.

The Book of Daniel highlights this pervasive theme in Israel's history: Humankind's power is no match for God's power. Because we find ourselves living in intimidating external circumstances does not mean we must abandon our belief in God and forgo a living faith. Daniel's life experience provides lessons in how to live within these tensions and how to be true to self and God while serving those in power over us.

The humane circumstances portrayed in the opening pages of Daniel's story belie some of the harsh realities of deportation, captivity, and exile. The conditions of detention in Babylon, while not disastrous, still presented severe challenges. While the period of indoctrination and training for Daniel and his associates seemed filled with the bland pleasantries of such cultural inducements as adjusting their dietary tastes to Babylonian fare and expanding the trainees' capacities for fine wines, the strategy of complete assimilation of the captives through a systematic plan of programming, enforcement, and employment remained at play.

All empires and nations have the capacity to transform conquered client nations into vehicles for their own ends. Assimilation is cultural, but not always political, integration where the levers of power are actually wielded by the conquered. But Daniel and his three associates—as in the case of Joseph in Egypt—were granted a measure of political power because they had proved themselves trustworthy servants of the empire.

Thus, the process of completely absorbing the exiles into Babylonian culture was a primary objective of Nebuchadnezzar and his successors. It was emblematic of a basic plan of training and social integration. By changing their names and their sensory tastes for food and wine, they would receive a complete makeover into the folkways of the Babylonians. Subsequent to receiving their training, they were expected to do what they were told and obey every command given them. As handsome, mild-mannered, intelligent men who fulfilled all the external requirements for service in the king's court, they were ripe candidates for a thorough makeover in service to the king.

However, meeting the external requirements for selection for service did not mean internal compliance. For Daniel and his three associates, complete assimilation into Babylonian culture did not mean their total assimilation into those social, political, and cultural systems demanding obedience and loyalty in matters of personal faith. It also did not mean that Daniel and his three friends lost their personal sovereignty. Their faith in God provided a measure of resistance and insulation, preventing the domestication and obliteration of their faith. That provides a profound lesson in having it both ways.[2] They all were willing to pay the price with their lives and would not be forced to choose between Yahweh and the imperial regency of Babylon. The sovereignty of Yahweh was realized in the religious autonomy of Daniel and his three friends. The Babylonian regency could not exact unmerited influence over the Israelites. Daniel and his associates became cultural and political insiders because they had won the trust of their regent sponsors and were granted positions of provincial authority while not surrendering their faith in Yahweh or their personal identities.

From the Outside Looking In to the Inside Looking Out:
You've Got to Serve Somebody!

What followed was a series of faith trials and tests that culminated in acts of compliance and resistance that dramatized the paradox and ironies of Daniel's situation. Customary readings of these texts view them as challenges for Daniel and his associates. They tested those patterns of social conformity and compliance that had established those patterns as behavioral precedents that were established for all future exiles. But the tests were also put to their hosts and involved testing the limits of imperial authority, the capacities of personal freedom, and the limits of exercising a monotheistic and foreign faith.

Faith Test One: What's in a Name? Abiding a Name Change but Resisting Complete Identity Change
Daniel 1:1-7

Changing a person's name is one of the first steps to changing a person's identity—another step in converting the outsider to insider. A name change signifies the complete authority of Nebuchadnezzar. The name *Daniel* means "God is my Judge." *Hananiah* means "The Lord shows grace." *Mishael* means "Who is what God is?" *Azariah* means "The Lord helps."[3] These are spiritual names that reference the Lord's grace and power.

Assimilating into new environs and cultures often requires a name change for the individual to fit in with the larger culture. It was not uncommon for Jewish people who came to America in the early twentieth century to abbreviate their Jewish names to names of Anglo origin. "Greenberg" was sometimes shortened to "Green." In the famous movie *Roots*, we see that a first step toward assimilation of Africans into American colonial life and culture occurred by changing their African names into Anglicized names. Kunta Kinte's name was changed to Toby. Likewise, Daniel's name was changed to Belteshazzar, which probably means something related to Babylon. The three Hebrew men had their names changed to signify their relationship to the Babylonians. It was not an uncommon practice with exiled or captive persons at that time to experience a name change. But it is also curious that the writer of Daniel seldom refers to Daniel by the name *Belteshazzar*.

Just as naming a child is a first step in defining a person, changing one's name is a first step in redefining that person. In the case of Daniel and his three associates, their name changes ultimately symbolized that they would be defined and their destiny controlled by their captors. Having their names changed would also mean that they would ultimately begin to name, describe, and define themselves in accordance with the culture and worldview of their Babylonian hosts, which is also a way of stripping from them any form of self-determination. In her book *Signs of a Prophet*, Morna D. Hooker reminds us that Jesus renamed Simon to Peter, signifying the rock. During the time of the preresurrection Jesus, Peter was anything but a rock. Hooker says that Jesus renamed Peter not to characterize what he was but what he was to become in the postresurrection faith community.[4]

The structure of the narrative affirms the name *Daniel* and is constantly referenced in relation to the man, which in some indirect way might suggest that Daniel himself never fully accepted his Babylonian name.

Faith Test Two: Refusing Sensory Seduction by Not Eating the King's Rich Food or Drinking the King's "Cheap" Wine

Daniel 1:8-21

The king's rich food would ingratiate the men to the king. The king's wine might anesthetize the men to all the painful changes required of them. The Babylonians sought to seduce them through their appetites so indoctrination would be easier. A standard practice at that time was to offer first portions of food and drink to idols, which in the minds of Daniel and his associates meant that the food and wine were also contaminated.

Daniel asked permission to opt out of the king's diet and challenged the chief official, with whom he had cultivated a trusting relationship, to accept his request to eat only vegetables and water. The chief official was afraid that the king would punish him if he granted Daniel's request and Daniel's heath failed. Daniel then put his request to the guard by asking that he test the young men by allowing them a vegetarian diet for ten days. The guard complied, and Daniel proved to be right. After ten days of vegetables and water, Daniel and his associates were leaner, healthier, and more alert than if they had eaten the king's food. The result was that

Daniel was able to answer the king's questions about his dreams with complete confidence, knowledge, and wisdom.

By refusing the king's rich food and wine, was Daniel also testing the rules of that system to determine its true limits? Perhaps, he thought, it wasn't so rigid after all, for if the system could be tried and plied to his own means and ends, he might establish a measure of personal sovereignty and autonomy that would not force him to compromise his faith. By passing his own dietary tests, he showed the Babylonians that there was a better and healthier way of existence than that proposed and imposed upon the exiles.

Faith Test Three: Petitioning the God in Heaven and Revealing the Meaning of the King's Dream

Daniel 2:1-13

King Nebuchadnezzar was disturbed that neither he nor any of his sages and seers could interpret the true meaning of his dreams. Outraged, the king threatened to annihilate all the sages, including Daniel and his friends.

Daniel 2:14-23

After discovering the king's threats, Daniel met the king's executioner and asked why the king was so angry. After learning the reasons for the king's anger, Daniel went directly to the king, begged for time to interpret the dream, and went to Hananiah, Mishael, and Azariah so they could ask for help from the God in heaven about the king's dream. Then, in a vision, God revealed the mystery for him. Daniel immediately praised God.

Daniel 2:24-47

Daniel then approached Arioch, the man appointed to wipe out all the incompetent sages. Daniel asked that their lives be spared and that he be taken before the king to interpret his dream. Before explaining the dream to the king, Daniel paid tribute to and credited the "God in heaven" for revealing the dream's meaning to him. Daniel provided a political interpretation of the dream's meaning and told the king that four future rulers and their inferior kingdoms will rise up in his existing kingdom; but the God in heaven will raise an everlasting, indestructible kingdom that will stand firm forever. Daniel assured the king that the dream had issued from God and that it could be trusted because he was a great God. God's revelation to Daniel was that even the political kingdoms would be accountable to God.

The king then bowed and honored Daniel, exalted him, lavished gifts on him, and made him ruler over all the province of Babylon and chief minister over all Babylon's sages. The king also appointed Daniel's three friends to administer the province while Daniel remained at the king's royal court.

Faith Test Four: Entering the Fiery Furnace and Refusing Spiritual Reduction by Bowing Down to the King's Golden and Graven Images

Daniel 3

King Nebuchadnezzar, excited by Daniel's interpretation of his dream and resonating with his reference to the huge statue whose head was made of gold, built a ninety-foot gold statue and issued an edict that everyone should worship it. At the sound of trumpets, the people were to bow to the gold statue; those who refused would be thrown in the fiery furnace. Shadrach, Meshach, and Abednego would not comply. When the king learned of their infraction, he confronted them; but they still refused to worship the gold statue even after being threatened again with death in the fiery furnace. Into the furnace they went, trusting that their God would deliver them. The prospects of being charred in the fire did not dissuade the three from keeping their faith in God. Warren Wiersbe reminds us that when God allows people to enter the fiery furnace of faith, God always has an eye on the clock and a hand on the thermostat.[5]

Gold is one of the few substances that never lose value in whatever form it comes. It can be smelted and melted but still remains pure gold. The Roman statesman Seneca once said, "Fire is the test of gold; adversity, of strong men."[6] The furnace would be heated seven times hotter than the customary temperature for charring the unchaste.

The king had hoped that his edict could be rescinded because he did not really want to put the men into the furnace, but even the ruler could not revoke the rule. When the men were thrown into the fire, they did not burn. They came out unscathed, and the king marveled at their God and their faith. It was a fire-tested faith that protects men and women from the scorching embers of unbelief.

Faith Test Five: The King's Tree Dream and Daniel's Vision of the Tree Cut Down; Refusing to Compromise the Sovereignty of God's True Revelation

Daniel 4

King Nebuchadnezzar had another dream; this one featured a large tree growing strong and tall until it touched the sky. It was beautiful and abundant, and all the wild animals found shelter in it. While lying in bed, the king saw a holy messenger who told him to cut down the tree and trim its branches and strip its leaves but leave a stump bound with iron and bronze. The holy ones had spoken, and the king called Daniel for interpretation.

Daniel told the king that the tree to be cut down was the king and that he would be driven away from his people to live with the wild animals. The stump of the tree symbolized his restored kingdom if he acknowledged that the Most High was sovereign over all the kingdoms on earth. The king was driven from his people as foretold; and finally, in God's time, he raised his eyes to heaven to acknowledge and praise the one true God. The king acknowledged the God in heaven and his righteousness and justness. Then the king was restored to his throne.

The sovereignty of God was demonstrated in the autonomy of his servant Daniel to speak divine truths to earthly powers. Nebuchadnezzar bowed before God as a show of acknowledgment of the power of Daniel's God.

Faith Test Six: The Meaning of the Handwriting on the Wall and Refusing to Compromise God's Revelatory Truth

Daniel 5

Nebuchadnezzar's son Belshazzar ascended the throne, succeeding his father. He sees handwriting on the wall and must summon Daniel for

About the Faith

From Faith Then to Now

Faith is a consistent theme in the Holy Bible. In order for your faith to work, you have to work your faith. God desires to restore faith in the people and demands that the people have faith only in God. Usually such faith requires a series of strength or tensile tests that will ultimately determine the outcome of human situations. Daniel and his three associates are members of the Biblical Faith Hall of Fame. Their steadfastness and determination to remain true to their God amid adverse and life-threatening conditions are lessons for people everywhere.

Much of our faith witness and power boils down to whether we possess the will and strength to hold on to faith and risk even our very own life during such times. In our journey with God, we will have our trials and tests by fire, our moments in the lions' den of persecution, and our other challenges. When we are ready to put life all on the line, we have reached the higher tiers of a living faith.

I once heard a story about a young man who was asked by his spiritual teacher to follow him into a river so that he could demonstrate a faith lesson. When they were standing in the middle of the river, the teacher asked the young man what he wanted more than anything else in life. The young man replied, "Faith, teacher. I want faith."

Suddenly the teacher pushed the young man under water and held him there almost to the point of drowning. Released, the young man flew out of the water bewildered, flailing his arms and gasping for air. "What did you want more than anything else just now?" asked the teacher. "I wanted air," said the young man. The teacher replied, "When you pursue faith like you want air, you will arrive at your place of longing."

Strong faith is an important lesson of Daniel and his three associates.

interpretation since none of the wise men, enchanters, diviners, or astrologers could interpret that handwriting. Daniel speaks the power of divine truth by telling him that his father was all-powerful but did not realize true power until he acknowledged God as sovereign over all the kingdoms of the earth. Daniel further warned him that because he did not humble his heart but set himself up against the Lord of heaven, the days of his kingdom would be numbered and divided and that he was found wanting. The king elevated Daniel to the third highest ruler in the kingdom, but doom came to Belshazzar. He was later slain by Darius and the Persians just as Daniel foresaw.

Faith Test Seven: Refusing to Worship King Darius; Praying to the Sovereign God for Help and Then Thrown to the Lions

Daniel 6

After the murder of Belshazzar, the mighty King Darius mounted the throne; and Daniel administered his portion of the kingdom with integrity and trustworthiness and without corruption. Jealousy of other administrators and satraps set in because the outsider became an insider and they found no fault with his leadership. They fashioned an edict warning that anyone who bowed down and worshiped any other god or human being except Darius would be thrown to the lions within thirty days.

After hearing the edict, Daniel went to his upper room, opened his windows toward Jerusalem, and prayed to God for help. Hearing of his affront to the king, the king's minions reported Daniel's infraction. Because of the edict and the pressure from the group of men, the king ordered Daniel to be thrown to the lions because he broke the law. However, the king believed that Daniel's God would rescue him.

Daniel entered the lions' den, and God found him innocent of charges. God locked the lions' jaws, and the next morning Daniel was freed from the den by the relieved and rejoicing king. From then on, Daniel prospered under the reign of Darius.

Live the Story

The sovereignty of Yahweh was demonstrated not only by God's acts of protection, vindication, and deliverance of God's faithful servants but also by the autonomy of Daniel and his associates. Their refusal to give in to the king's demands and threats revealed the true power of a living faith. God's sovereignty inspires human autonomy. Humans' power to overwhelm the faithful cannot compete with God's power to rescue them from perishing. Exile conditions need not mean a completely servile disposition where we compromise our deepest beliefs in order to fit in with our external circumstances. Serving those who occupy the political throne does not mean we must dethrone our allegiance to the one who sits on the eternal throne.

When we sometimes feel like we are living in exilic conditions, God may test our faith by putting us through a series of trials. The tension between serving those who rule us and keeping a measure of personal integrity and autonomy may be an important part of maintaining a living faith under exilic conditions.

In what ways have you found yourself tempted to compromise or negotiate the terms of a living faith in daily situations?

How have you managed the tension of externally serving those who have dominion over you while keeping your allegiance to God internally?

In what critical ways have these tensions been manifested in your life as a member of a faith community?

To be in and not of the world is a daily challenge for Christians and other believers. How does one live out this challenge day to day?

In what other ways does the experience of Daniel and his three associates reveal to you the importance of keeping the faith?

1. *The Jewish Study Bible*, Adele Berlin and Marc Zvi Brettler, eds. (New York: Oxford University Press, 2004), 1643.

2. Walter Bruggemann, *The Prophetic Imagination*, Second Edition (Minneapolis, Minnesota: Augsburg Fortress Press, 2001), 3. Bruggemann discusses the importance of prophetic ministry as the development of the alternative consciousness to the dominant culture. Such consciousness serves to criticize in dismantling the dominant consciousness and realities that lead to the domestication of the human spirit and its propensity for freedom and justice.

3. *The NIV Study Bible* (Grand Rapids, Michigan: Zondervan, 2011), 1417.

4. Morna D. Hooker, *The Signs of a Prophet* (Harrisburg, Pennsylvania: Trinity Press, 1997), 39.

5. Warren W. Wiersbe, *The Wiersbe Bible Commentary: Old Testament* (Colorado Springs, Colorado: David C. Cook, 2007), 25.

6. http://www.quotationspage.com/quote/24424.html (accessed 8-6-13).

6.

The Limits of Earthly Kingdoms and the Power of a Sovereign God

Daniel 7–12

Daniel's visions and prophecies for Israel—God controls history and human destiny and works through people and circumstances, so righteousness ultimately overcomes sin.

Claim Your Story

Have you ever heard the voice of God? I know a Christian writer who reports that one day when he was boasting over and over about his own great talents and successes, he heard the voice of God chuckle and ask, "Now, just who did these great things?" The man claims he heard God's voice with his ears, not just with his mind and heart through a dream. And he was chastened.

Stories of meetings with angels and near-death experiences appear in print with increasing frequency. Contacts with heavenly beings and the afterlife suddenly seem common. Like in times of great illness, many people show God's compassion and extend a healing hand to someone who has done nothing to create their present circumstance. Other reported incidences show God's help in times of unexpected and even unrecognized danger. Careful consideration of these reports often can uncover something in addition to a timely rescue. With some regularity, persons are not actually innocent victims, but perpetrators of their own difficulties. In these cases, the communications and interventions from God are actually calls to return to correct behavior.

Do you have a wise counselor in your life? Someone who always helps you with life's problems and gives you effective suggestions for making decisions and proper behavior? Sometimes God's help comes from important people in our lives. They seem to have a clear vision of how to live according to God's plan.

Regardless of how you receive messages from God—directly from God's voice, in dreams, or from a godly emissary—you can understand Daniel and his colleagues. Daniel knew to eat healthy foods and obey the one God. He was able to witness that to anyone watching. He also knew how to counsel others about God's will for them. Foreign kings and fellow Israelites alike benefited from watching and listening to Daniel.

Enter the Bible Story

In the books of Ezekiel and Daniel, we see the power of divine visions revealed to servants chosen as spokespersons of hope and redemption to the people of Israel. One trait of God's continuing revelation in human history is the freedom of God, the sovereign manner in which God chooses those who will speak to the people for him as they meet the challenges of daily living. Although the people of God have suffered for and by their sins, it is God's desire to restore the covenant relationship of mutual respect, reciprocity, and dignity with humans.

In the Book of Ezekiel, the people's role in bringing exile on themselves through their sinfulness and lack of faith is a prominent theme; but the Book of Daniel focuses more on the power of deliverance of God's servants from the limitations of their external conditions and punitive power of their overlords. Overcoming their exilic condition and external circumstances by maintaining steadfast faith in a sovereign God is also an expression of God's power and sovereignty and the sustenance of God's people.

That God would use visions of God's choosing and thus reveal them to interpreters of God's choosing is yet another example of God's absolute sovereignty. The God of heaven did not forget the people and worked to redeem and restore them even in their exile. The reach of God is unlimited, the power of God unknowable, and redemption and deliverance by God is certain.

In the end, no earthly power fashioned by human hands can determine the ultimate outcome of the people. Their harsh social and spiritual circumstances were no indication as to what God will ultimately do to transform their exile into freedom. The justice and righteousness of God will prevail in all things that will overcome all sin.

Visions of the Four Beasts: The Earthly Kingdoms Will Rise but Will Not Defeat the People of God!

Daniel 7

The causes of exile were partly religious and partly political. The conquest of God's people in Israel and Judah was particularly satisfying for the conquerors because it demonstrated the impotence of the sovereign God in heaven. Worldly conquerors from Nebuchadnezzar to Alexander the Great revealed that the people of God needed more than faith and a prayer to stop their marching armies. Religious sovereignty in the minds of vanquishers was no match for the political power of earthly authorities. But the truth of the matter is that God and the people of God win out in the end. Faith and prayer do matter. Divine justice prevails over human injustice, and righteousness and peace triumph over enmity and war.

The God in heaven ultimately rules over the kingdoms of this earth, and Daniel's visions again confirmed the truth of God's power over worldly power. Humankind, in its quest for earthly rule and absolute dominion over everything, has not mastered the lessons of ignoring and defying God. Kingdoms of this earth will all eventually wither and perish, but the kingdom of God and the people of God will endure forever. In his book *God and Empire*, John Dominic Crossan tells us of the tension between the kingdom of God and the kingdoms of this world, both claiming sovereignty, both claiming eternal power; one of heaven and earth and the other of earth whose pretensions to power claims authoritative reach even beyond the heavens.[1]

The four beasts of which Daniel spoke are the four earthly kingdoms that would rise in power and providence (7:1-14). These beasts lived to devour human flesh while living in unholy pursuit of false idols. They were perpetually engaged in the deification and exaltation of the earthly rulers that pretended supremacy over the sovereign God of heaven and earth. These empires ruled by terror and violence. They perpetuated distinct patterns of subjugation that caused people to abandon hope in the higher, invisible God. Only the holy people of God, including Daniel and his three associates, kept the faith. These empires were not content until all sacred things were completely demolished and desecrated and all vestiges of true faith and belief were vanquished unto the ends of the earth.

The four beasts represented each of the following: the empire of Babylon with a head of gold, the Medo-Persian Empires represented by the breast of silver; the empire of Greece symbolized by the belly of brass and the conquests of Alexander the Great; and the Roman Empire with legs of iron that was different from all others.[2] These four powerful kingdoms waged war against God's holy people and will defeat them. The fourth kingdom, Rome, spoke against God and oppressed God's holy people. Then the earthly sovereign greatness of all the kingdoms under heaven was given to the holy ones of the Most High. God granted those kingdoms over to the people of God and granted the people eternal reign and everlasting victory.

The symbol of beasts was fitting given the violent nature of these kingdoms. It was also appropriate for rulers who instinctively lived out their reign of power in a predatory, bloodthirsty fashion. Like wild beasts that consume and devour their prey to satisfy their unquenchable appetites, the four kingdoms rose to become indomitable forces of world power in ancient times from Babylon in 626 B.C. to Rome and to the fall of Jerusalem in A.D. 70 and the decline of Rome in A.D. 641.

Both Israel and Judah were small, insignificant nations in comparison to these empires; but their belief in a sovereign God who demanded a solemn faith from his people made them formidable foes to their enemies. The might and power of Israel and Judah were amazing given their diminutive resources. The one final ruler of the four empires became very strong and subdued the other three kings. But the court issued its judgment and the kingdoms were handed over to the people of God (7:15-28).

Two Kingdoms Butt Heads: The Clash of the Ram and the Goat and Daniel's Interpretation of the Vision

Daniel 8:1-27

The Ram (Medo-Persia) was attacked and battered by the Goat (Greece) and had its two horns shattered. The goat became very great, but at its apex the large horn was broken off with four horns growing in its place. The larger horn represented Alexander the Great. Daniel was told that the four horns that would replace the large horn that was broken off represented four less powerful kingdoms. Then, a master of intrigue would arise and bring devastation and desolation to the holy people, causing deceit to prosper and wretchedness to prevail. This master would be destroyed but not by human power. This clashing of powers signified the futility of the destructive power of earthly kingdoms. What thrived by the sword would die by the sword, and Daniel was troubled by what he saw.

For Daniel, the vision was of the end of time. Daniel was confronted by Gabriel and was informed that the two-horned ram represented the kings of Media and Persia and the longhaired goat was the king of Greece. The horn that snapped so that four arose in its place represented the four kingdoms that would rise from one nation but of lesser strength than the first. This new ruler would be the master of cunning and deception. He would wreak havoc and destroy the holy ones. Even then, he would not be destroyed by another kingdom or by human hands.

The Prayer of the Righteous

Daniel 9:1-19

As Christians, we believe there is power in prayer. Through our Judeo-Christian heritage, we find fervent examples of prayers offered on behalf of God's people. Daniel was completely exhausted by the dream and then launched into a heartfelt prayer to God. Referencing God in everything that he did was the bedrock of his faith and a reason for his survival in Babylon. His faith allowed him to face the limitations of his earthly circumstances but allowed him the elasticity to adapt to a variety of changing conditions under the reign of numerous rulers.

We see that a distinct pattern developed in Daniel's prayer life. The king had a dream and could not find interpreters. Daniel was summoned to interpret the dream. Daniel always invoked and consulted God prior to every action and followed God's entreaties with disciplined obedience. Daniel never shrank from speaking truth to Nebuchadnezzar, Belshazzar, and Darius though they wielded the power of life and death over him. Instead he spoke divine truth in accordance to the vision and revelation of God. Then he would fervently pray, confessing (9:4b-10) his people's sins of unfaithfulness and their subsequent punishment by defeat and exile. Daniel's confession cited how the people ignored the prophets and other messengers that God had sent them over the years (9:11-14). Daniel confessed the role of his people in bringing onto themselves the shame of isolation and disempowerment but asked that God deliver them as God did in Egypt. Daniel humbly pleaded to God for mercy and forgiveness (9:15-19). His righteous prayer of confession was filled with compassion and humility and the recognition of his personal sins and those of his people and the affirmation that God was the sovereign who had the power to grant much-needed forgiveness.

Seventy Weeks Prophecy

Daniel 9:20-27

While Daniel was still praying and confessing his sins and the sins of Israel, Gabriel approached him. Gabriel told him that Daniel and his people have seventy weeks to stop their rebellion, to stop sinning, to cover wrongdoing, to bring eternal righteousness, to set up prophetic vision, and to anoint the most holy place (9:22-24). "Daniel believed, from his knowledge of Jeremiah's prophecy, that a period of seventy years was decreed for the desolation of Jerusalem (9:2; cf. Jer. 25:11f.)."[3] Gabriel exhorted him to gain wisdom from this knowledge. He was told that it will be seventy weeks from the moment that the word goes out to rebuild Jerusalem and an anointed leader prince would lose the support of the people. The army of the future leader would destroy the city and the sanctuary, and his end would come in a flood. The seventy weeks was to be a time of preparation for the final verdict on the fate of the exiles.

About the Christian Faith

Tradition and Practice of Faith

Faith often requires disciplined and sustained practice. Usually that practice occurs under conditions of stress and duress. Those conditions can be brought on by persecution, misunderstanding, conflict, and a variety of circumstances that put us at odds with our environment and the culture in which we exist.

The Christian faith has demanded sustained practice in the development of theology and belief systems and in the organization and perpetuation of the Christian church. Any reading of Christian history will reveal the various trials by fire undergone by the believers who have fought the good fight and have lived out those faith claims even at risk to their own lives.

This tradition of faith and practice goes back to the beginning of the Bible to people like Abraham, Moses, Elijah, Joshua, Deborah, David, and the prophets. It can be viewed in the ministry of our Lord and the works of Paul the apostle, Lois and Eunice, and other servants. This practice of faith can be viewed in the lives of thousands of people, well known and lesser known, who have said "here I stand," and have pressed forth in confidence and knowledge of the goodness and righteousness of God.

As we live our lives each day as part of a faith community, it is important to remember that practice completes our faith. The continuing demands of life show that faith will always meet the greatest tests under conditions of fire. In order for our faith to work, we must work our faith. God calls and challenges each of us to give strident and steadfast witness to God's love, redemption, and salvation in human history.

The experience of Daniel and all the other great and faithful servants in history are part of our continuing legacy. Upon their shoulders, we stand as servants and witnesses of a God of love and justice in the march of human history.

The Vision of a Man: The Servant of God Was Greatly Treasured

Daniel 10

Daniel fasted from eating meat and wine and mourned from the frightening visions and devastating images of the continued oppression of his people by various empires. A man confronted him, and his words put Daniel into a trance. The man touched Daniel, and he rose to his feet to hear these words, "Daniel, you are greatly treasured. . . . Stand up, because I've been sent to you. . . . Don't be afraid. . . . I've come to help you understand what will happen to your people in the future, because there is another vision concerning that time" (verses 11-14).

"Someone who looked like a human being" touched his lips, and then Daniel opened his mouth and exclaimed that the vision bothered him and he couldn't stay strong because of it. He lamented that he had no strength and could barely breathe. But the vision touched him again and said, "Don't be afraid. You are greatly treasured. All will be well with you. Be strong!" (verse 19). Daniel felt strong and knew that he could go on. The one who looked like a human being vowed to go back to fight the leaders of Persia and Greece and said that no one would stand with him against these leaders except Michael, one of the highest leaders in the Persian army.

Daniel's fatigue after all these visions symbolized the depletion of the exiles on the last remnants of their faith. How long will the suffering continue? How long must the people endure the tyranny of the earthly rulers? How long must they undergo humiliation at the hands of foreigners who had invaded their homeland and destroyed the arch symbols of their true and living faith?

A Vast Empire Divided and the End of an Arrogant King

Daniel 11

The drama of earthly kingdoms' quests for hegemony continued as they divided and conquered their enemies and were divided and conquered by their foes. Their divisions emerged not only from the outside pressure of warring enemies but also from the vast internal contradictions and conflicts that led to their demise. It was difficult for empires to maintain the resources they needed to build great monuments and feed great armies while expanding their geographical boundaries. Such imperial ascendancy came at a great price; and as many scholars of history have revealed, the internal divisions that emerged from managing such vast empires eventually gave way to total collapse. The weakening brought on by internal and external conflict are lessons of power that empires in history have not learned. Three more kings would emerge from Persia and the fourth would be richer.[4] A warrior king would emerge whose kingdom will be broken.

Soon after the death of Alexander the Great in 323 B.C., his generals divided his empire into four parts, two of which, Egypt and Syria, were under the rule of the Ptolemies and Seleucids. The Holy Land was controlled by Egypt in the Ptolemaic dynasty from 323 to 198 B.C. and was later governed by the Seleucids of Syria from 198 to 142 B.C.[5]

The arrogant king could do whatever he wanted with God's people, and he continued the fateful patterns of regent narcissism displayed by his predecessors. It is self-glorification leading to self-denigration (verse 36). The political purposes of previous empires continued into the latter empire; these purposes were to wield power at any cost, subjugate enemies, and expand the frontiers of their kingdoms to the ends of the earth. The ultimate purpose was to have all vassals of the state cower and worship the kings as gods. The faith of God's people teaches the importance of genuflecting to no god but Yahweh. Yahweh alone is the supreme and sovereign God and there can be no other gods.

The paradox of human worship versus God worship was still a prominent theme in Israelite history as it is in the Book of Daniel. The "cult of the emperor" dominated as a political reality and continually clashed with the Israelite belief that no power is greater than God's power. The haughtiness that issued from earthly governance and the aggregate annexation of political power from conquered nations was repeatedly trumped by the spiritual power of a few dedicated individuals, a spiritual remnant who clung to their faith, resisted the amalgamation of their religious beliefs, and refused to bow down to the gods of this world. God's sovereign hegemony was climaxed in the faithful servant's spiritual autonomy.

The challenge was to serve one's rulers but also to keep one's faith and live out the demands of compliance amid the imperatives of religious sovereignty and belief. Daniel's experience dramatized the reality and tensions of living in these two realities.

The Breaking of the Holy People's Power Is Complete and the Servant of God Will Be Rewarded!

Daniel 12

There is a happy ending for the people of God who remain steadfast in faith. While earthly kingdoms rule and exile occurs for the people of God so they can learn a lesson in trusting God, God will have the final word on what life will become for the people. Daniel, whose obedience to

God shone as brightly as the stars in heaven, remains the prototype of how faith can be used to interpret the political times and glorify spiritually the God in heaven. God as the ultimate interpreter and decider of human history will provide the proper analysis of the things that are to come.

The handwriting on the wall was not a forgery. The divine truths spoken by the servant of God did come to pass, and the servants did not compromise their faith. They were raised to positions of governance. They did not get big egos. They served their masters and kept their humility, but kept a sovereignty of faith that became a hallmark of religious ideals of the Jewish people and Christians who claim that spiritual heritage is a vital part of their own spiritual identity. Even Christ himself referred to the prophecies of Daniel (Matthew 24:15).

In the end, the servant will be allowed to rest and stand to receive his reward in the final days. Peace will prevail, and the kingdom of God will be on earth. No more divisions, strife, warfare, and bloodshed. The people of God will take their rightful place among the peoples of all the earth. Not only will they become positive examples of resolute faith but also faithful witnesses to the restorative, redemptive, and saving power of the God of human history.

Live the Story

Usually our journey of faith is lived in many chapters, requiring that we sustain our belief in God over long periods of time and under varying conditions of trial. When in your journey of faith and witness have you endured trials that challenged your faith? These trials come in many forms such as in family life, in our vocational and professional lives, and even our church and faith community. We often think that life challenges are harder for people without faith. True, but that does not diminish what it takes for believers to face the trials.

Sometimes, in life's daily transactions, people ask that we relinquish or compromise our religious beliefs to perform tasks that will aid them in a political crisis. Practical necessities at times demand that we do this, but we should not refrain from praying and looking to God for the ultimate answers to all of our human predicaments. The problem is that we often leave God out of our considerations.

Although today we tend to have a compartmentalized understanding of God and the world, the truth is that God is Lord of the universe. God's watchful eye and concern extends even into the political realm with a prophetic concern for compassion, truth, and justice for all people. God is not only concerned about our worship of God, but how we practice that worship in the execution of justice, truth, love, and hope amid human circumstances and conditions. Sometimes we meet harsh opposition in the expression of our religious values and beliefs and we shrink in fear and doubt. At other times, we are like Daniel. We will not back down from our allegiance to God even if it means our own end.

Daniel and his three associates provide a good example of how to serve a governing God by living a true and autonomous faith. It is a lesson that we can cherish amid those faith challenges outside and inside our various places of existence.

In what ways does your personal and professional life parallel the experience of Daniel?

In what ways have you held to your faith amid challenging life choices and circumstances?

What tensions did you experience in the transactions of serving man and serving God, and how did you resolve them?

What sacrifices have you been willing to make to remain steadfast in your commitment to Christ and your service to the church?

Have you ever experienced persecution for your religious beliefs? What was your response?

What are the takeaway lessons of Daniel and his three associates?

1. John Dominic Crossan, *God and Empire* (San Francisco: HarperCollins, 2007).

2. Cambyses (530-522 B.C.), Gaumata (522) and Darius (522-486) and Xerxes I (486-465), *The NIV Study Bible* (Grand Rapids, Michigan: Zondervan, 2011), 1434. Also see William Sanford LaSor, David Allan Hubbard, Frederick Wm. Bush, *Old Testament Survey*, Second Edition (Grand Rapids, Michigan: William B. Eerdmans, 1996), 576-582.

3. *Old Testament Survey*, 579.

4. *The NIV Study Bible*, 1434.

5. Ibid., 1435-1436.

Leader Guide

People often view the Bible as a maze of obscure people, places, and events from centuries ago and struggle to relate it to their daily lives. IMMERSION invites us to experience the Bible as a record of God's loving revelation to humankind. These studies recognize our emotional, spiritual, and intellectual needs and welcome us into the Bible story and into deeper faith.

As leader of an IMMERSION group, you will help participants to encounter the Word of God and the God of the Word that will lead to new creation in Christ. You do not have to be an expert to lead; in fact, you will participate with your group in listening to and applying God's life-transforming Word to your lives. You and your group will explore the building blocks of the Christian faith through key stories, people, ideas, and teachings in every book of the Bible. You will also explore the bridges and points of connection between the Old and New Testaments.

Choosing and Using the Bible

The central goal of IMMERSION is engaging the members of your group with the Bible in a way that informs their minds, forms their hearts, and transforms the way they live out their Christian faith. Participants will need this study book and a Bible. IMMERSION is an excellent accompaniment to the Common English Bible (CEB). It shares with the CEB four common aims: clarity of language, faith in the Bible's power to transform lives, the emotional expectation that people will find the love of God, and the rational expectation that people will find the knowledge of God.

Other recommended study Bibles include *The New Interpreter's Study Bible* (NRSV), *The New Oxford Annotated Study Bible* (NRSV), *The HarperCollins Study Bible* (NRSV), the *NIV and TNIV Study Bibles*, and the *Archaeological Study Bible* (NIV). Encourage participants to use more than one translation. *The Message: The Bible in Contemporary Language* is a modern paraphrase of the Bible, based on the original languages. Eugene H. Peterson has created a masterful presentation of the Scripture text, which is best used alongside rather than in place of the CEB or another primary English translation.

One of the most reliable interpreters of the Bible's meaning is the Bible itself. Invite participants first of all to allow Scripture to have its say. Pay attention to context. Ask questions of the text. Read every passage with curiosity, always seeking to answer the basic Who? What? Where? When? and Why? questions.

Bible study groups should also have handy essential reference resources in case someone wants more information or needs clarification on specific words, terms, concepts, places, or people mentioned in the Bible. A Bible dictionary, Bible atlas, concordance, and one-volume Bible commentary together make for a good, basic reference library.

The Leader's Role

An effective leader prepares ahead. This leader guide provides easy-to-follow, step-by-step suggestions for leading a group. The key task of the leader is to guide discussion and activities that will engage heart and head and will invite faith development. Discussion questions are included, and you may want to add questions posed by you or your group. Here are suggestions for helping your group engage Scripture:

State questions clearly and simply.

Ask questions that move Bible truths from "outside" (dealing with concepts, ideas, or information about a passage) to "inside" (relating to the experiences, hopes, and dreams of the participants).

Work for variety in your questions, including compare and contrast, information recall, motivation, connections, speculation, and evaluation.

Avoid questions that call for yes-or-no responses or answers that are obvious.

Don't be afraid of silence during a discussion. It often yields especially thoughtful comments.

Test questions before using them by attempting to answer them yourself.

When leading a discussion, pay attention to the mood of your group by "listening" with your eyes as well as your ears.

Guidelines for the Group

IMMERSION is designed to promote full engagement with the Bible for the purpose of growing faith and building up Christian community. While much can be gained from individual reading, a group Bible study offers an ideal setting in which to achieve these aims. Encourage participants to bring their Bibles and read from Scripture during the session. Invite participants to consider the following guidelines as they participate in the group:

Respect differences of interpretation and understanding.

Support one another with Christian kindness, compassion, and courtesy.

Listen to others with the goal of understanding rather than agreeing or disagreeing.

Celebrate the opportunity to grow in faith through Bible study.

Approach the Bible as a dialogue partner, open to the possibility of being challenged or changed by God's Word.

Recognize that each person brings unique and valuable life experiences to the group and is an important part of the community.

Reflect theologically—that is, be attentive to three basic questions: What does this say about God? What does this say about me/us? What does this say about the relationship between God and me/us?

Commit to a lived faith response in light of insights you gain from the Bible. In other words, what changes in attitudes (how you believe) or actions (how you behave) are called for by God's Word?

Group Sessions

The group sessions, like the chapters themselves, are built around three sections: "Claim Your Story," "Enter the Bible Story," and "Live the Story." Sessions are designed to move participants from an awareness of their own life story, issues, needs, and experiences into an encounter and dialogue with the story of Scripture and to make decisions integrating their personal stories and the Bible's story.

The session plans in the following pages will provide questions and activities to help your group focus on the particular content of each chapter. In addition to questions and activities, the plans will include chapter title, Scripture, and faith focus.

Here are things to keep in mind for all the sessions:

Prepare Ahead

Study the Scripture, comparing different translations and perhaps a paraphrase.

Read the chapter, and consider what it says about your life and the Scripture.

Gather materials such as large sheets of paper or a markerboard with markers.

Prepare the learning area. Write the faith focus for all to see.

Welcome Participants

Invite participants to greet one another.

Tell them to find one or two people and talk about the faith focus.

Ask: What words stand out for you? Why?

Guide the Session

Look together at "Claim Your Story." Ask participants to give their reactions to the stories and examples given in each chapter. Use questions from the session plan to elicit comments based on personal experiences and insights.

Ask participants to open their Bibles and "Enter the Bible Story." For each portion of Scripture, use questions from the session plan to help participants gain insight into the text and relate it to issues in their own lives.

Step through the activity or questions posed in "Live the Story." Encourage participants to embrace what they have learned and to apply it in their daily lives.

Invite participants to offer their responses or insights about the boxed material in "Across the Testaments," "About the Scripture," and "About the Christian Faith."

Close the Session

Encourage participants to read the following week's Scripture and chapter before the next session.

Offer a closing prayer.

1. Finally Comes the Prophet:
The Call and Commissioning of Ezekiel
Ezekiel 1–3

Faith Focus
God's word is creative and powerful and sets into motion God's activity, which involves meeting people where they are and sending someone to move them toward redemption and salvation. God reveals his glory to rebellious humans and sends them someone to lead them back to God.

Before the Session
Pray for God's guidance during your time of preparation, and pray for the participants in your IMMERSION Bible study group. Read the Scriptures for Session 1 and jot down any questions or insights that emerge for you. Consider what questions might emerge from your group. Read Chapter 1 of this study book. Before the participants arrive, write the Faith Focus on a markerboard or a large sheet of paper for all to see. Have markers and several large sheets of paper available.

Claim Your Story
Read or review highlights of "Claim Your Story." Ask: Which experience resonates most with you? Why? When have you felt alone, isolated, or exiled? What was it like? When have you felt as though you were isolated or exiled from God?

Enter the Bible Story
Discuss "The Reality of Exile"
Review highlights of "The Reality of Exile: But How Can We Sing the Lord's Song in a Strange Land?" In this section, the writer mentions two kinds of crises, personal and social, that lead to a feeling of isolation or exile. What are some personal crises that have caused you or someone you know to have such feelings? What are some social crises that you think might lead to such feelings? How do you see hope in such situations? Read aloud Psalm 137:1-4. What do you think it would be like to be conquered and physically moved from your homeland to another country? What do you think God's role would be in such a situation? Why would it be impossible for the exiles to "sing the LORD's song"?

Illustrate Images in Ezekiel 1
Read aloud Ezekiel 1. Tell the group to form teams of two. Give each team a large sheet of paper or posterboard and some markers. Tell them to create an illustration of one image described in Ezekiel 1. After a few moments invite teams to show their illustrations and tell why they chose their image. Ask: What does the image say to you about God? about Ezekiel? What sounds are mentioned in Chapter 1? What do they suggest to you? What do the images and sounds say to you about the power of God? What is Ezekiel's response to the vision from God?

Explore Ezekiel's Commission

Have the group form three teams. Assign Ezekiel 2:1 and the section "Stand on Your Feet and Listen to God!" to team one; Ezekiel 2:3-4 and the section "Walk With Your Feet to the People of God" to team two; and Ezekiel 2:4-5 and the section "Stay on Your Feet and *Speak* the Truth of God!" to team three. Tell the teams to review Chapters 2 and 3, identify the phrases that fit their assignment, and list them. Have them review highlights of their assigned sections. When they have finished these tasks, tell them to discuss the following questions: How do you see your team's assigned commission being carried out in contemporary life? How do the commissions to Ezekiel speak to you about contemporary Christian life?

Reflect on Judgment and Hope

Have the group form two teams. Assign Ezekiel 2 to one team and Ezekiel 3 to the other team. Tell the teams to review their assigned chapter and identify statements of judgment and statements of hope. Have them discuss the following question: How do you respond to the chapter's statements of judgment? Where do you see hope? Have each team share highlights of their discussions with the entire group.

Live the Story

Read aloud the Faith Focus for Chapter 1. Review highlights of the section "Live the Story." Have participants find a partner. Invite them to share with one another times they have felt alone or isolated. What was it like? Invite them to share experiences of "being at home." What does this feel like? Who in your life or in the life of someone you know has been the voice of "home" to you? Who has helped you hear more clearly the voice of God?

Have the group reassemble and ask them to prayerfully consider their personal responses to the following question: What do you think you might do this week to feel "at home" with God? Close the session with silent prayer followed by the Lord's Prayer.

2. "The Fire This Time!"
Ezekiel 4–24

Faith Focus
Ezekiel says to the people that because of their rebellion against God, God will bring destruction to Jerusalem and exile to the people. God's holiness requires that God judge sin and allow disobedient people to live with the consequences of their unfaithfulness, yet God's love and mercy compel God to offer to repentant people hope for new life.

Before the Session
Pray for God's guidance during your time of preparation, and pray for the participants in your IMMERSION Bible study group. Read the Scriptures for Session 2 and jot down any questions or insights that emerge for you. Consider what questions might emerge from your group. Read Chapter 2 of this study book. Before the participants arrive, write the Faith Focus on a markerboard or a large sheet of paper for all to see. Have index cards on hand for the closing devotional activity.

Claim Your Story
Have someone read aloud the story of the writer's daughter in "Claim Your Story." Invite participants to share their own stories about themselves or about family members or friends who did not heed warnings about an action and suffered the consequences. Ask: What do these stories say to you about human nature? Do you see anything positive about doing something even though you have been warned about the consequences? If so, what? Explain. What do your experiences say to you about God and about our responses to God?

Enter the Bible Story
Reflect on Prophetic Judgment
Review highlights of the section "A Sign for the House of Israel: Burn, Baby, Burn!" Say something like: Our writer reminds us of Ezekiel's prophetic view: "God is completely fed up with the people; tired of their iniquity and refusal to heed his commands; tired of them promising devotional obedience while only showing rebellious disobedience." How do you respond to this view of God? Why do you think the prophet Ezekiel understands the misfortunes of the people of Israel to be God's judgment? What hope, if any, do you see in proclaiming this view of God?

Create "Sign-Acts"
Have the group form two teams. Assign Ezekiel 4 to team one and Ezekiel 5 to team two. Have the teams review highlights of the assigned chapters and information about them in "A Sign for the House of Israel: Burn, Baby, Burn!" After a few moments of review, tell the teams to create a "sign-act" to portray some contemporary life situation or news event in which human behavior needs

to be transformed. One team will present their "sign-act" and the other team will try to guess what it represents. Ask: In today's world, how do we realize the need to pay attention to needed change in our lives and culture? What sign-act might represent an action in your life that would help you grow closer to God?

Make a "Backpack" List

Read or review highlights of Ezekiel 12 and the information in "Backpacks for Exile." Tell the group to imagine that they must leave the United States and live in a different country. They must put important items in their backpack for the journey. Invite them to make a list of what they would put into the backpack. When they have finished, invite them to tell about their list. Say something like: The baggage sign-act in Ezekiel 12 warns that the people will go into exile. Ask: What might the image of the baggage or backpack and the pending exile say to you about your relationship with God?

Consider a Word of Hope

Read aloud Ezekiel 11:14-21. Ask: How does this chapter differ from most of the others in this section? How does it offer hope to a defeated and exiled people? What images stand out for you? What does the Scripture passage say to you about God's desire for relationship? What does it say to you about judgment? about God's grace?

Live the Story

Read aloud the opening paragraph of "Live the Story." Ask: How do you think God's "burning love holds out the possibilities of redemption"? What have been the "hot stove" experiences in your life? Invite participants to reflect prayerfully as you read aloud the questions included in this section. Pause for a moment after each question. Invite participants to share insights if they would like to do so, but do not pressure them to talk. Ask: How do you think God invites you to move forward in your faith? Invite participants to write a response on an index card that they will carry with them in the week ahead. Tell them they will not have to share what they have written with anyone. Close with a prayer that offers thanks to God for salvation and new beginnings when we have failed.

3. Let the Neighboring Nations Beware!
Ezekiel 25–32

Faith Focus
Ezekiel prophesies that God will bring judgment and destruction to those who harm God's people. All peoples and earthly powers are subject to God's power and are instruments in God's pursuit of divine justice.

Before the Session
Pray for God's guidance during your time of preparation, and pray for the participants in your IMMERSION Bible study group. Read the Scriptures for Session 3 and jot down any questions or insights that emerge for you. Consider what questions might emerge from your group. Read Chapter 3 of this study book. Before the participants arrive, write the Faith Focus on a markerboard or a large sheet of paper for all to see. Have masking tape, paper, pens or pencils, three sheets of posterboard, markers, old magazines, and glue on hand.

Claim Your Story
Read aloud "Claim Your Story." Ask: When have you experienced both conflict and support in a close relationship? What was it like? How do you respond to the idea that it is OK for you to have conflict, but not for others to criticize or have conflict with your close friend or family member? How do you respond to this idea as a way to think about the relationship between the people of Jerusalem and God?

Enter the Bible Story
Play "Agree or Disagree"
Ahead of time make x's on opposite sides of the floor with masking tape—one x for "agree," two x's for "disagree." Tell the group that the writer describes Ezekiel's understanding, God's people, and neighboring nations of God's people. Read aloud each of the following statements. Invite participants to stand in the disagree or agree area as they respond to the statements. Some may want to stand at some point between the two areas. When everyone has taken their position in response to a statement, invite them to tell about their response. After you have read aloud all the statements and everyone has had an opportunity to respond, ask: What did you find challenging? Which statement made most sense to you? Why?

- God ultimately wants to reclaim and restore his people to a relationship where they honor God first and then abide by God's entreaties and commands.
- If they follow God's commandments and honor their covenant with God, their misery can be temporarily alleviated and then permanently eliminated. They will no longer be judged, condemned, and punished perma-

nently as exiles and can finally live the spiritually and materially rewarding lives that God meant for them to live.
- God delights neither in the destruction of his people nor the jeering of their
  enemies who mock their devastation.
- God is against those who are against God's people and will bring judgment
  and destruction to them.
- All peoples and earthly powers are subject to God's power and are instruments in God's pursuit of divine justice.

Discuss Celebrating the Misfortunes of Others

Review highlights of "Putting the Surrounding Nations on Notice." Ask: How
do you think the people of Judah and Jerusalem felt about the prophet's words
of God's judgment against neighboring nations who mocked them? How do you
respond to the story a church member shared about her classmates having a
party when she failed biochemistry in medical school? What insights or feelings
do you have about this story? How do you think it illustrates Ezekiel's understanding of God?

Have a Bible Study

Have the group form three teams. Assign one of the following sections of
Ezekiel to each of the teams: Ezekiel 25; Ezekiel 26–28; Ezekiel 29–32. Tell them
to review the Scriptures and the material about them in the chapter. Have them
discuss the following: What nations are mentioned? What is the complaint against
the nations? What do the Scriptures say to you about the power of God? the justice of God? God's relationship with the people of Judah and Jerusalem? How
do you respond to Ezekiel's views of God as expressed in these Scripture
passages?

Create Illustrations of Restoration

Have the groups remain separated in the three teams established for the
Bible study above. Give each team a sheet of posterboard, markers, old magazines with pictures, and glue. Tell the teams to read Ezekiel 28:25-26 and to create an illustration of the images of restoration using the art supplies. When they
have completed, have each team tell about their illustration. Ask: How do you
see God's hope and restoration in our world today? in your own life?

Write an Oracle

Review the information in "Oracles." Tell participants to review the oracles
discussed in previous activities. Have them read Ezekiel 28:25-26 again and
write an oracle telling about God's restoration in our world today. When they have
finished, invite them to read their oracles aloud. Ask: How do you think we can
be part of the vision of God's restoration?

Live the Story

Consider Steps Toward Restoration

Read the section "Live the Story." Ask: When have we been reluctant to lend a helping hand to others in our world? in our nation? in our communities? in our church? Why do you think we are sometimes reluctant to help? To stimulate further discussion, read aloud the questions included in this section. After a time of discussion, invite participants to pray silently about one way they can offer help to someone they know during the week ahead. This might be a family member, a friend, an acquaintance at work or church. Close the session with the following prayer:

God, we thank you for Ezekiel's insights about your power, your justice, and your desire for restored relationship. We also thank you for your guidance about how we might live as your people and help you in restoring wholeness to our world. In Christ we pray. Amen.

4. "I Want You Back!"
Ezekiel 33–48

Faith Focus
God offers the people an invitation and a way to return to God and the Temple. All peoples and earthly powers are subject to God's power and are instruments in God's pursuit of divine justice.

Before the Session
Pray for God's guidance during your time of preparation, and pray for the participants in your IMMERSION Bible study group. Read the Scriptures for Session 4 and jot down any questions or insights that emerge for you. Consider what questions might emerge from your group. Read Chapter 4 of this study book. Before the participants arrive, write the Faith Focus on a markerboard or a large sheet of paper for all to see. Locate a recording of "Bridge Over Troubled Water" by Simon and Garfunkel. Have equipment available to play the song. You will need several sheets of posterboard, markers, and masking tape. Before the group gathers, place a strip of masking tape on the floor to represent a bridge. Make sure it is long enough for all the participants to stand on it at the same time.

Claim Your Story
Play the song "Bridge Over Troubled Water" by Simon and Garfunkel. Ask: What memories, thoughts, or feelings does this song evoke in you? Read aloud "Claim Your Story." Ask: When have you experienced troubled water? Who was the bridge over the troubled water for you? What troubled water do you see in our community? in our nation? in our world?

Enter the Bible Story
Discuss Hope in the Midst of Destruction
Read or review highlights of the opening paragraphs in "Enter the Bible Story." How do you respond to the prophet's view that God will do a new thing when the Temple has been destroyed and Jerusalem is in ruins? How do you think the people heard the promise? How do you think you would hear it if you were living with the destruction?

Create a Poster of God's Watchman or Lookout
Have the group form teams of three or four. Tell the teams to read Ezekiel 33:1-10 and the section "Closing the Gap." Give each team a sheet of posterboard and markers. Tell them to discuss the following questions: How do you respond to the image of the prophet as God's "lookout"? What is the message of hope in this Scripture? Who do you see as the "lookouts" in our culture? What do you think the message of hope would be to our world? Tell the teams to make a simple sketch or drawing of a contemporary lookout. Write words or phrases about the message of hope that this lookout might offer to the world. Have each

team tell about the poster they have created. Ask: How do you think God's "look-out" is like a bridge over troubled water?

Talk About the Good Shepherd
Read aloud Ezekiel 34:11-16. Ask: How does this image speak to you? What thoughts or feelings do you have about the good shepherd image for God? How does this image contrast with the image of the shepherd in verses 1-10 and 17-31? Read aloud verses 17-31. Ask: What images of the provision and protection given by the "good shepherd" speak most to you? Why? When have you experienced God's presence, comfort, care, and safety? What was it like for you?

Explore Visions of Restoration
Have the group separate into four teams. Assign each team one of the following Scriptures featuring visions of restoration: Ezekiel 36:1-15 – mountains and cities; Ezekiel 36:16-38 – hearts and spirit; Ezekiel 37:1-14 – dry bones; Ezekiel 37:15-28 – reunited kingdom. Tell each team to read their assigned Scripture and the material related to it. Have them discuss the following questions: How do you think the people of Ezekiel's time heard these visions of restoration? How do you hear them? How do they speak to you about God's desire to restore us and all creation? After the teams have had time to discuss their Scriptures, invite them to share highlights of their conversations with the reassembled group.

Consider the Visions of a Restored Temple
Tell the group that Ezekiel 40–47 focuses on the restoration of the destroyed Temple and the worship rituals. The Temple had been understood as God's dwelling place among the people. What might they have thought about God's presence with them when the Temple was destroyed? What hope would the images of a restored Temple and religious practice offer to them?

Live the Story

Take Steps Toward God's Vision
Read aloud the following: "Every step is another opportunity to listen to God and choose God's way. Every step is a chance to take the bridge over troubled water and find the life-giving waters promised by the prophets. Every step takes us closer to God's vision for all of creation. Every step leads to God." Play the song "Bridge Over Troubled Water" softly as background music. As the music plays, invite participants to step onto the "bridge" (the strip of masking tape that you placed on the floor before the group arrived). Tell them prayerfully to consider the following questions as they step onto God's bridge over troubled water. As you survey the experience of Ezekiel's calling the people back to God and behold God's ultimate plan of return and restoration from the experience of exile, what parallel lessons can you draw in your personal experience? What can you do this week to take steps that will bring you closer to God's vision for your life?

5. From the Outside Looking In to the Inside Looking Out: You've Got to Serve Somebody!
Daniel 1–6

Faith Focus
Daniel and his three companions are in exile. Human power is no match for God's power; adverse and hostile circumstances present no obstacle for God's presence and activity among God's faithful people.

Before the Session
Pray for God's guidance during your time of preparation, and pray for the participants in your IMMERSION Bible study group. Read the Scriptures for Session 5 and jot down any questions or insights that emerge for you. Consider what questions might emerge from your group. Read Chapter 5 of this study book. Before the participants arrive, write the Faith Focus on a markerboard or a large sheet of paper for all to see. Have a variety of art supplies on hand: posterboard or large sheets of paper, old magazines, glue, scissors, and colored markers.

Claim Your Story
Read or review highlights of "Claim Your Story." How do you respond to the writer's story about his son's feelings of isolation when he was injured and unable to play with the team? When have you felt similar to his son? What was your situation? How did you get through it?

Enter the Bible Story
Discuss "A True and Living Faith"
Read or review highlights of Daniel 1 and the section "A True and Living Faith." What thoughts or feelings do you have about Daniel and his friends wanting to maintain the dietary guidelines that were part of their faith in Yahweh? What risks do you think were associated with this request? What does their choice to maintain the practices of their faith and to participate in the king's court say to you? What situations in our culture or in our history seem similar to you?

Consider Names
Invite participants to tell about their names. What do their names say to them about their identities? about their ancestors? Have a participant read aloud Daniel 1:6-7. Review highlights of "Faith Test One: What's in a Name?" Ask: If you were going to change your name, what name would you choose? Why? What feelings or thoughts do you have about someone else changing your name?

Reflect on Dreams
Invite participants to tell about their personal experiences with dreams. Ask: Do you dream? What do you think about dreams? Are they more like nonsense

or do they offer insights to you? If so, how do they help you sort through feelings or actions in your daily life? What dreams have been significant for you? Why? Have the group form two teams. Assign Daniel 2 and the section, "Faith Test Three" to team one. Assign Daniel 4 and the section "Faith Test Five" to team two. Tell the teams to read their assigned Scriptures and the material about them. Have them discuss the following questions: What does this Scripture say to you about the king? What does it say to you about Daniel? How does it speak to you about your own faith? Invite the teams to share highlights of their discussions with the reassembled group.

Illustrate Biblical Texts

Have the group form three teams. Give each team a large sheet of paper or posterboard, old magazines, scissors, glue, and colored markers. Make the following assignments: team one – Daniel 3 and "Faith Test Four"; team two – Daniel 5 and "Faith Test Six"; team three – Daniel 6 and "Faith Test Seven." Tell the teams to read their assignments and to create an illustration of the Scripture and its message to us using the art supplies you have given them. When they have finished their illustrations, tell them to discuss the following questions: What does the Scripture say to you about God? about the king and his court? about Daniel or his friends? How does it speak to you about your faith? Invite the teams to tell the reassembled group about their illustrations and the highlights of their team discussion.

Live the Story

Read aloud the focus statement and the section "Live the Story." Ask the questions in this section to stimulate discussion. Close with a prayer asking for God's strength and guidance as you seek ways to grow in your allegiance to God, especially when you are challenged by the culture or when you are tempted to compromise your faith.

6. The Limits of Earthly Kingdoms and the Power of a Sovereign God
Daniel 7–12

Faith Focus
Through Daniel's visions and prophecies for Israel, we see that God controls history and human destiny. God works through people and circumstances so that righteousness ultimately overcomes sin.

Before the Session
Pray for God's guidance during your time of preparation, and pray for the participants in your IMMERSION Bible study group. Read the Scriptures for Session 6 and jot down any questions or insights that emerge for you. Consider what questions might emerge from your group. Read Chapter 6 of this study book. Before the participants arrive, write the Faith Focus on a markerboard or a large sheet of paper for all to see. Ahead of time gather the following supplies: several large sheets of white paper or posterboard and markers, a markerboard and markers.

Claim Your Story
Read aloud the section entitled "Claim Your Story." How do you respond to the idea that the man mentioned at the beginning of this section actually heard God's voice? How do you think we can hear God's voice? What experiences do you have of recognizing God's voice? How do you respond to the idea that God speaks to others through you and your life?

Enter the Bible Story
Illustrate the Visions
Have the group form two teams. Give each team a large sheet of white paper or posterboard and some markers. Assign Daniel 7 and the section "Visions of the Four Beasts" to team one. Assign Daniel 8 and the section "Two Kingdoms Butt Heads: The Clash of the Ram and the Goat" to team two. Have the teams read their assigned material and create an illustration of the visions in their chapter. Tell them to discuss the following questions: What does the vision say to you? What feelings or thoughts does it stir up within you? How does it speak to you about power? about humans? about God? What hope do you see in the vision?

Write a Prayer
Have participants form teams of two or three. Tell them to read Daniel's prayer of confession in Daniel 9:1-19 and to write a contemporary version of the prayer that relates to our culture and life. Invite participants to read their prayers aloud. Ask: What does Daniel's prayer say to you about human beings? about God? about humility and confession? about forgiveness? How do you respond to Daniel's understanding that the misfortunes of defeat and exile are due to the people's unfaithfulness to God?

Reflect on "Greatly Treasured"
Read aloud Daniel 10:1-8. Invite participants to think about times in their lives when they have felt exhausted by misfortune, illness, loss, or other trying situations. After a few moments of silent reflection, read aloud verses 18-19. Ask: How have you found strength during times of hardship? How did Daniel respond to these words: "Don't be afraid. You are greatly treasured. All will be well with you. Be strong!"? How would it affect you to hear these words during your times of hardship? What do they suggest to you about God's presence during difficult times?

Consider Conflict, Politics, and Power
Review highlights of Daniel 11 and the section "A Vast Empire Divided and the End of an Arrogant King." What insights, thoughts, or feelings does this chapter prompt in you as you consider events in the contemporary world?

Brainstorm Ideas and Images of "End Time"
Invite participates to say aloud words or phrases that come to them when they hear "End Time." List these responses on a markerboard for all to see. Review highlights of Daniel 12 and the section "The Breaking of the Holy People's Power Is Complete and the Servant of God Will Be Rewarded!" Ask: How do you see hope and reward expressed in this passage? What does the phrase "steadfast in faith" suggest to you about your daily life as a Christian?

Live the Story
Read aloud the section "Live the Story" and the Faith Focus for this chapter. Invite participants to reflect prayerfully on the questions at the end of this section. Read them aloud, then pause for prayerful reflection. Close this time of prayerful reflection by praying aloud the following:
God of the universe, help us remain steadfast in our faith. Help us claim for ourselves the knowledge that you are with us and that you act for good in all circumstances. Amen.

IMMERSE YOURSELF IN ANOTHER VOLUME

IMMERSION
Bible Studies

Available at Cokesbury and other booksellers

AbingdonPress.com

BKM126600001 PACP01238834-01